THE
BETWEEN
TIME

Savoring the sacred moments
of everyday life

DAMARIS ZEHNER

D1194325

TWENTY
THIRD
PUBLICATIONS

www.23rdpublications.co

ACKNOWLEDGMENTS

Some of these stories and meditations appeared over the last five years on the website InternetMonk, and I am grateful to moderator Mike Mercer and all the commenters for their feedback. I thank my husband, Andy, and daughters Kate and Hannah for their proofreading and helpful suggestions, and my daughters Jenny and Sarah for tolerating my demands on the communal computer and my occasional insistence on silence. I also thank Jeff Dunn, editor extraordinaire and the motive force behind this collection, for his faith that it could be done.

I dedicate this book to my mother, who long ago introduced me to the joys of essays and to a taste for contemplative Christian literature. She can no longer understand this dedication and would be surprised by it if she could, but still she has my deepest gratitude.

Damaris Zehner

TWENTY-THIRD PUBLICATIONS
1 Montauk Avenue, Suite 200, New London, CT 06320
(860) 437-3012 » (800) 321-0411 » www.23rdpublications.com

ISBN: 978-1-62785-110-7
Library of Congress Catalog Card Number:
Printed in the U.S.A.

≡[CONTENTS]≡

The Between Time

The paradox of the Christian life is that we live in a between time. Our race exists between the original creation and the unveiling of the new heavens and the new earth. Our brief years between birth and death can seem endless as we await salvation. We hold on with faith between God's promises and their distant fulfillment. Life breaks us and heals us, healing us to break us again. We never quite fit in the world and in our skins, because they are always changing, and so are we. We've left, but we're not there yet. This is the between time.

Scripture expresses the same awareness of the between time. A concordance search for the phrase "How long?" will yield laments throughout the Old and New Testaments. How long will God forget us? say the psalms. How long before God will restore us? How long will God remain hidden, and how long will the wicked exult? Habakkuk wonders how long he will cry for help and God not hear him. Revelation asks how long before God will judge and avenge.

God hears our lament and answers it. The Book of Isaiah is a perfect and consistent expression of the universal human experience of dissonance and the unfolding of God's glorious redemption. But when will that redemption be complete? Although Scripture cautions us that with God "a day is as a thousand years," it also tells us that Jesus is coming quickly.

That's good news to me. I suppose I'm an expert on living in the between time. Much of my life has been spent in the no-man's-land of travel—on airplanes, ships, trains, cars, cargo trucks, even canoes. The sense of being no longer here but not yet there underpins my experience of the cosmos. Travel was in my family: my father was a diplomat in the Foreign Service who moved to new posts every few years. I also spent two years in the Peace Corps in Liberia, where I met my husband. Later he and I and our children lived in Kyrgyzstan for seven years. Since returning, we have no plans to move. Still, though, life moves around us. Our children grow and leave; we age; people are born and die—even staying put we're traveling, and we're not there yet.

I'm still on my journey of faith as well, although recently I have found, if not a harbor, at least a rest stop. As a child I was baptized and confirmed in the Anglican Church, but while I remained content with Anglicanism, the church changed around me, and I discovered in my twenties that I no longer belonged. My husband came from a different background, so we compromised by attending evangelical Protestant churches for many years. We began to feel—to hope, desperately—that there was more to our historic faith than we were finding in the churches we attended. Our seven years in the mission field in Kyrgyzstan strengthened our conviction that do-it-yourself Christianity, churches with stages rather than altars, and the sovereignty of individual interpretation of Scripture were not for us. Thus began a time of searching that culminated in our entrance into the

Catholic Church in 2011. These stories, written over the last five years or so, trace aspects of the between time of faith and finally recount my sense of having found a place of peace from which to continue my journey.

When we were getting ready to move to Kyrgyzstan as mission workers, I took an anthropology course at a local Bible college. One thing especially struck me. The professor explained that the Genesis account of Adam and Eve's first disobedience was really the story of broken relationships: with nature, with self, with others, and with God. In these areas, we know stress and sin. In these areas, Christ brings us healing through his incarnation, death, and resurrection, revealed in the sacrament of communion, which reunites the fruits of nature, the work of human hands, and the grace of God.

The professor's point made sense to me, and I've decided to use it as the structure for this book. In Part One I write about our relationship with nature, in Part Two our relationship with ourselves and others, and in Part Three our relationship with God. These three sections explore the mixed experience of the between time. Perhaps I should have written them entirely from one perspective or the other; I could have focused only on the burdens and disappointments of everyday life, or I could have written only a triumphant declaration of faith. But most of us don't live in one state or the other. We are tossed up with the wave tops and splashed down into the troughs every day we spend negotiating the deeps. Separating the struggles from the triumphs paints a false picture of the between time we all live in. This book bears witness to the brokenness of sin, but it also expresses faith in the ultimate healing of all God's creation.

When the Lord restored the fortunes of Zion,
we were like those who dreamed.
Our mouths were filled with laughter,

our tongues with songs of joy.
Then it was said among the nations,
"The Lord has done great things for them."
The Lord has done great things for us,
and we are filled with joy.
Restore our fortunes, Lord,
like streams in the Negev.
Those who sow with tears
will reap with songs of joy.
Those who go out weeping,
carrying seed to sow,
will return with songs of joy,
carrying sheaves with them.

PSALM 126

Part One

NATURE

CHAPTER ONE

The Good Land

Only recently did I discover that the monastic vows of Saint Benedict included the vow of stability: poverty, chastity, obedience, and stability—staying in one place. This was a revelation to me. By the time I was thirteen, I had lived on four continents, in five countries. Since the age of twenty-five, I have added another nine years overseas, in Africa and Asia. Even when I stayed in one country for a while, I moved from house to house. There were some constants in my life, but stability as Saint Benedict understood it was entirely absent.

Nine years ago my family and I came back to Indiana from Central Asia and bought an old brick farmhouse in the middle of cornfields. I prayed then, and I still pray now, that I would be taught the strange skill of staying put. There would be no more escaping from myself by moving to another house or around the world. Eventually I would have to face the ups and downs of the people around me—I can't be always a casual stranger, comfortable as that is. I would have to tackle the long-term tasks that never arise if I move every year, such as painting walls, cleaning the oven, and dealing with people I've offended. I would have to learn to be content with this place, this weather, these plants and trees and soils.

Living in one place has not turned out to be a prison sentence, though; it's a friendship, a long-term relationship that grows in love as it grows in familiarity. Every time I go outside and look, "the heavens are telling the glory of God; the firmament proclaims his handiwork" (Psalm 19:1). God is revealed through the place that God has given me: "a good land, a land of brooks of water, of fountains and springs, flowing forth in valleys and hills, a land of wheat and barley, of vines and fig trees and pomegranates, a land of olive trees and honey, a land in which you will eat bread without scarcity, in which you will lack nothing... And you shall eat and be full, and you shall bless the LORD your God for the good land he has given you" (Deuteronomy 8:7–10).

After staying put in this good land for almost a decade, I've learned its moods and many faces. I've noticed the movement of the sunrise and sunset along the horizon as summer changes to winter. I know where the wild berries grow and where the kingfisher perches. I've become accustomed to the improbable screeching of the peacocks on the farm south of us. I know which dogs will chase my bike and which roads are best to ride on. I know who is related to whom, who shears sheep and who sells eggs, who has been married or widowed. And I am myself known.

But a passive failure to move isn't all that I'm called to. There is a virtue not just to **staying** where I am but to **being** where I am—and that's the real challenge. Too often I'm not really here. I stare at the computer (as I do now), or read a book, insulated from the uniqueness of the place I live. Sometimes even when I'm working in the garden or hiking or bike riding outside, my body occupies a vague, in-between world while my mind is editing the past or worrying about the future.

A few years ago I came across this parable: A prisoner spent many years in a cell. He prayed daily that God would appear to him. All the rest of his time he stared out the tiny window at a patch of sky and imagined the world and people outside. Eventually he died and met God face to face. "Lord," he cried in reproach, "for years I prayed that you would come to me, and you never did." "My son," God replied, "I was in that prison cell every day; but where were you?"

Saint Benedict wasn't talking just about my body staying put. My mind, too, must be stable. Both mind and body must be together in one place in order to practice the presence of God, as Brother Lawrence would put it. God will never be in the imaginary places, the greener grass springing from my discontent—God is too real to occupy those vague lands—and neither will I. This place where I am is the only place I can meet God. This old farmhouse is the doorway to the kingdom of heaven.

God, you have planted me here.
Teach me to be present and to be whole.
May I grow in gratitude in this good land,
and may I meet you and know you in the paths of my daily life.
Amen.

≡[CHAPTER TWO]≡

The Blessings of Boredom

"In an era of hyperstimulation it can be difficult for people to realize that enlightenment comes not by increasing the level of excitement, but by moving more deeply into calm. There is a kind of monotony that is not boredom but paves the way for a more profound experience."

That quotation leaped out at me from a book called *Sacred Reading: The Ancient Art of Lectio Divina*, by Michael Casey. It expresses well something I've thought as a child, a teacher, a writer, a parent, and a Christian: boredom is a blessing. From what we call boredom, as from dirt, great things can grow.

Not all cultures complain about boredom or even seem to have a concept of it. I never knew anyone to complain specifically of boredom in Liberia, for example, although people would wander away from something they didn't find interesting. After seven years in Kyrgyzstan, I never found a Kyrgyz word that meant "boredom." The Kyrgyz can say something is not interesting, or that they are not interested in it—they can curl up and go to sleep in the middle of a party without self-consciousness—but their language can't express the pervasive state of being that is modern Western boredom. Nor do I recall much description of boredom in classical or medieval writing.

Here and now, however, people seem to devote vast amounts of energy to fighting off boredom. According to Merriam-Webster, boredom is "the state of being weary and restless through lack of interest." Most people these days would take it further and define boredom as nothing stimulating to be doing right this minute. A hundred years ago, a teacher's greatest dread might be an epidemic disease, or the stove-heated schoolhouse burning down; teachers today dread boredom, laboring breathlessly to make their classes interesting, amusing, and stimulating—to prevent weariness and restlessness. Parents used to worry about their children's health and moral growth; parents today worry about scheduling activities for every waking moment their children are not in school. Early printers were concerned to make their books accurate and blot-free; printers today cram every page with multi-colored images, sidebars, fancy fonts, even scratch-and-sniff patches and motion-activated music recordings. Boredom seems to be the worst thing out there.

Sometimes, of course, our sense of boredom may be an accurate and helpful response to poor conditions. People whose lives are purposeless, lonely, uncreative, and oppressed will be bored—and they're right to be. Boredom, like pain, is in that case the warning that something is wrong and that change is necessary. Even if these people can't change their conditions,

they are challenged to change their response to them and find
purpose, work, and service within the life they are leading now.

There is a less healthy cause of boredom, though: entitlement.
Or to put it more bluntly, being spoiled. If people believe that
amusement is a right, then anything that doesn't seem immediately amusing to them is an infringement of that right. Even
though most people are never told that they have the right to
be amused, they have absorbed that idea from the tensely smiling teachers surrounded by posters, mobiles, videos, toy boxes,
stuffed animals, activity centers, manipulatives, computers—
baubles and bling everywhere. They figure out that just listening
to one person reading the news isn't good enough when every
station competes to fit in as many scrolling headlines, captions,
and insets as possible without completely obscuring the report-
er. Every new device that comes out screams that it connects
faster, does more, has more, is louder, brighter, more colorful,
more fun—and you deserve it!

The danger is that children—or adults—who are always busy
never have time to discover anything new. They rush from task
to task, driven by a frantic sense of urgency. If you asked them,
they would complain about the urgency—"I'm always so busy;
I have all these plans I don't have time for; I wish I had time
to think, to grow..."—but they've become habituated to it. And
when the urgency stops, the resulting "state of being weary and
restless through lack of interest" takes over. Their jangled nerves
can't stand the quiet, and immediately they identify the strange
feeling of empty time and space as boredom and hence as bad.

But that strange feeling of empty time and space is fertile
ground for creativity. Are you old enough to have had a real
summer vacation? To remember the long, hot days kicking
yourself back and forth in the swing, complaining to your mother about how bored you were? And then what came next? All
your youthful energy had to go somewhere. You decided to dig

a hole to China, perhaps, and although you never got to China, you found interesting worms and rocks and had fun filling the pit up with water from the hose and playing in the mud. You built a tree house. You spent hours studying an anthill. Or maybe you finally got out that model plane set that you hadn't had time for during the school year and discovered a lifelong fascination with aeronautics.

The feeling of empty time and space is the *blessing* of boredom, not the curse. In boredom we reach the ends of ourselves and find how limited we are. In boredom we can hear God speak and have the time and space to respond instead of burying God's call under the avalanche of amusement we're used to. The quotation I began with says just this: monotony paves the way for a more profound experience.

For thousands of years, the great religions have had much to say about holy boredom. Monastics, whether Christian, Buddhist, or Hindu, understand the disciplines of silence and divesting oneself of baubles and bling. The people who live close to the earth and notice the seasons learn to appreciate the "monotony" of the passage of time. And we can too—we can train ourselves to embrace holy boredom.

To do so we have to give up our rights, especially our right to be amused, and accept that everything comes from God's hand.

We have to discipline ourselves to abstain from too much stimulation. We have to acknowledge that "multitasking" is a delusion and that behind all the stuff we're racing to do is the sin of pride.

We have to be more attentive to natural rhythms—not because nature is divine, but because nature is not us. It takes humility to accept the sameness of every year, the alternations of bounty and scarcity, without complaining or thinking we have to crank everything up to eleven.

We have to habituate our shredded nerves to stillness, slowness, and calm. This means not swearing if the computer takes ten seconds instead of five to boot up, and not honking if the car ahead doesn't start the second the light turns green. It means learning to sit in the garden at least a few times a week without mowing or weeding (a hard one for me). It means being grateful for being stuck with nothing to do from time to time.

Ironically, the people who are the least bored are not those who have the most distractions. They are the people who can be content with empty time and space. Not only are these contented people not bored, they are also not boring. Think of that.

Lord of peace and patience,
empty me of the pride of busyness,
and fill me with delight when I find you
in the empty time and space
so feared by the frantic world.
Amen.

=| CHAPTER THREE |=

Nature and Nature's God

I f I advertised a photo contest on the theme of nature, these are the sorts of pictures I'd get: ripe berries hanging by the side of a path; clear, warm water and white sand; brilliant fall leaves outlined against a blue sky; a cardinal in the snow; the view from a mountain ridge of lush valleys beneath.

I'd be happy with those pictures. I find the natural world—the living and un-living things that exist without or even despite us people—to be heartbreakingly beautiful. I enjoy the fierceness of life and the endurance of things. It's restful not to matter to nature; it's a pleasant contrast to the tangle of human relationships in which I seem to be an important strand.

But these pictures are also nature: the ruins of a forest, up-ended by tornado or hurricane; blackened hillsides after a wildfire's gallop; drifts of snow only half concealing the frozen carcasses of cows; lampreys, leeches, maggots, and ticks; earth-quake, flood, drought, blight, plague, extinction, and extremes too hostile for our frail frames. Nature is beautiful, but it is also uncaring toward human beings. And not just human beings—existence in general seems to be a dangerous, wasteful, heartless process in which death and consumption dog the heels of birth and life.

I am told to consider nature in order to understand God, and I find that a bit problematic. Scripture tells me that creation is one way God's nature is revealed to us; as far as the power and beauty go, I can accept nature as a revelation of God, but what do I do with the parasitism and death? There are people—denizens of a wealthy, comfortable society largely insulated from natural forces—who seem to believe that nature itself is god and are content that it should be so. That doesn't work for me. My faith is founded on the conviction that God is a Person who loves humankind, who answers prayers. Nature is impersonal; if an animal eats me or I eat an animal, it's all the same to nature. Scripture tells me that God is not willing that any should perish; nature is content to produce millions of offspring in order to have a few dozen survive. I don't know what I am supposed to learn about God from nature, or exactly how I am to relate to creation.

Our relationship with nature and nature's God is profoundly baffling, but it seems to me there are two chief mistakes we can make in thinking about it. First, we assume that nature exists for our sake. I can't accept that. It exists for God's purposes and for its own sake. If a tree falls in the forest and there is no one there to hear it, of course it makes a noise. Only the most self-absorbed navel-gazer believes that the human ear, not the rabbit ear or the snake ear or the ear of God, must be the receptor of noise for it to exist. It does seem that God has put us in a special relationship to nature, but it has its own existence beyond our opinions of it. And its existence does not always make allowances for ours.

The first time I went to the Rockies, several decades ago, I sat on a massive mountainside at 12,000 feet altitude. Although there was no chance I would fall—it was steep but not precipitous—I was frozen with terror. It's hard to describe what the terror was; I only know that I was aware of the mountain beneath me as the body of a vast creature that might shrug me off at any moment, as a horse would shrug off a fly. I could almost feel it breathing. It was in some ways a valuable feeling, as any revelation is, but I still clutched handfuls of grass in each fist as I sat there exposed on its flank. To the mountain I was not the crown of creation; I was a bug.

The second mistake is the opposite of the first: instead of thinking we are all-important within nature, some people assume that we are not a part of nature at all, that we are a separate order of creature instead of a link in the food chain like algae and leopards. Again, there's an element of truth in this—we are different in many ways from the animals, vegetables, and minerals that surround us—but for good or ill we exist on this planet as they do; we are still strands in the web.

When I was in high school, I spent two summers hiking and camping with the Audubon Society. The leader I had both of those years was a devoted, knowledgeable woman, but she felt—tragically—that she and all human beings were pollutants in the natural world, foreign objects irritating the perfect processes of nature. She would get infuriated with us for our impact, slight though it was, on the world around us, as if our being there had defiled it. The owl who left its pellet under a tree or the chipmunk who dug a hole between the roots didn't spoil the perfection of the surroundings, according to her, but our footprints did.

On one hike in the mountains of West Virginia, I paused in

a shady glade. The others were a few minutes behind me; I enjoyed the brief solitude. A ray of light, almost palpable in the humid air, broke through the leaves and rested on a mossy stump. The sunlight on the moss seemed to me an icon, a window into truth, and I laid a penny on the stump in homage to its beauty, as I would an offering on an altar.

The rest of the group crunched and rustled into the clearing. Suddenly—"Oh, my God!" shouted our leader in disgust. "Look at this! Who did this? Who left a penny here? Why can't people just leave nature alone for other people to enjoy?" My hiking companions wandered over to see what she was talking about, but I stayed still and kept my mouth shut. I knew what she was looking at. To her, my homage was not offering but littering.

So how should we relate to nature? We are not in control of it, but we are still enmeshed in it. That is true of all creatures, of course, but we thought we had a special relationship to God, nature, and ourselves. However, we're not the conquerors we like to imagine, at least in this fallen world. A brief burst of wind or cold or heat or tectonic shift shows us how weak we actually are. This is a paradox of our existence: we are powerful but also weak; physical, but also spiritual; made in God's image, but also fragile, at the mercy of the planet on which we live. We are part of the natural order but still separated from it by our unique self-consciousness. We rely on a loving God who cares for us as a mother cares for her child—the same God who is a refining fire, vaster than the empty reaches of space and more powerful than an earthquake or hurricane.

I don't know what nature does or should reveal about God except that the Lord of creation will not be contained by our pretty pictures, subdivisions, and churches. We are desperately anxious to reduce nature to screensavers and God to a teddy bear, but the wildness of both won't let us. And I'm glad of that. I don't want a tame God, and while this fallen world of death and competition daunts me, I am confident both it and my understanding of it will be healed, and "the wolf also shall dwell with the lamb, and the leopard shall lie down with the goat...and a little child shall lead them" (Isaiah 11:6).

What can I know about you,
Lord of all creation?
You are too great for my understanding,
too beautiful for my gaze.
Teach me to trust in your gentleness
as well as to fear your power;
give me faith that one day, in this world of struggle,
the perishable will be clothed in the imperishable,
mortality in immortality;
death will be swallowed up in victory,
and all will be well.
Amen.

≡{ CHAPTER FOUR }≡

The Resurrection of Hope

One of our angora goats had twin kids. It was a cold day, below freezing. The babies were wet and small and frail. We left them alone for a little while, to let the mother take care of them, but when we returned to check on them, they were sprawled, limp and unconscious, on the cold shed floor.

My daughter Jenny had stayed home from school to keep an eye on the goats, and she jumped into action. We got a hairdryer and rags. We dried them and rubbed them, but we couldn't seem to warm them up. We called the vet; then we moved the babies into the house.

We keep the house pretty cool, and we hadn't ever tried to push the furnace up to eighty degrees. But we did then. We took turns roasting our legs over the heat register in the floor, holding the floppy babies in a kind of rag hammock over our laps while warm air blew on them from underneath. Plastic bottles filled with warm tap water banked them in on either side.

An ear twitched. One eye opened briefly. It was working; but was it going to be enough?

When the vet arrived, the babies were still so cold that he couldn't get their temperatures to register on his thermometer. He gave them a cortisone shot and a fifty-fifty chance of pulling through—fifty-fifty for the stronger one, less for the other. "You have to get their temperatures up," he told us. Jenny ran upstairs and got the family thermometer—*erstwhile* family thermometer—and we took temperatures every half hour.

Time seemed alternately to drag and fly. All that morning and afternoon we took turns holding the kids.

One of them raised her head! Then the other did. Faint mews emerged from the curly bundles. Finally, they started to butt their heads into us and try to suck on anything warm.

The pace picked up. We gave them warm water mixed with molasses in a little shot syringe—molasses cures everything in goats. The strong one's—Heidi's—temperature reached 100, and we rejoiced. Almost an hour later little Hope's temperature did the same. We bundled them together in a box over the register, then moved their large and anxious mother into the entryway of the house. At that point the dog and three cats also got anxious.

It is not much fun to milk a skittish angora goat with a sore, swollen udder, who has six-inch horns that seem always to be at the eye level of the milker. It took both of us, and we didn't get much, but the babies drank it up. All that afternoon we followed the same routine, clambering over the old child gate to get to the nanny goat, wrestling her into a corner, milking her while trying to keep her hoofs out of the little bucket, getting covered in everything one associates with barnyards. My other children got home from school and helped. Finally my husband arrived with formula and rubber nipples. The babies filled their stomachs and fell asleep.

Taking turns sleeping downstairs, trying not too successfully to keep the rest of the house clean, helping the flippy-floppy babies as they slip on the linoleum in their desperate quest for mother's milk—this is how our time has been spent. Today, Hope and Heidi are walking, nursing, staggering back into their cardboard box to curl up together and sleep—even showing some curiosity about the tiny world of the entryway. Hope's hind legs still splay a bit, but she's got a fierce will and will get right back up if she falls down. They will live.

I would probably have given up. Jenny was the one who named the kid Hope. I never seem to have much hope that things will turn out well. Hoping is painful, because it always implies uncertainty. If we knew everything was going to be all right, we wouldn't have to hope. I find it hard to embrace uncertainty, to live with sorrow and worry and pity. In my heart of hearts, I thought that it would be better if the kids died quickly. That way I could mourn and move on, keeping my heart hard and whole and protecting myself from having to care.

Because caring is exhausting. It reminds me of my helplessness. Many times there isn't a happy outcome to things you care about. I don't think I was born with a hard heart, but over the years I've offered up desperate prayers that were not answered—not that I could see, anyway. People I loved killing themselves with alcoholism; friends in poor countries dying of diseases that should have been curable; babies wasting away with hunger; women abused by their husbands who are themselves desperate; dogs stoned by uncaring children who have nothing better to do. I see these things, and I'm helpless. The terrible things go on happening. We love the story of Lazarus, but not every brother who dies is miraculously restored to his loving sisters. It's better not to indulge hope.

But today, for once at least, Hope is up and wobbling around the entryway, staggering to her mother, and nursing while her little helicopter tail goes round and round in ecstasy. I must keep this answer to prayer alive in my mind, next to all the seeming silences and refusals of God. Why he answers as he answers is a mystery. My job is to accept and trust, and, as my daughter showed me, to nurture Hope.

God, I ask to know;
you tell me to trust.
Open my heart to the pain of love,
and give me strength to bear the agony of hope.
Amen.

CHAPTER FIVE

Lazarus Still Died

He was a young man when he was raised from the dead. What happened then? Maybe a year or two later he caught some bug and died of diarrhea. Maybe he lived until the destruction of Jerusalem by Titus and was killed by an angry Roman soldier. Or maybe he died peacefully in bed, full of years. But the thing is, Lazarus died.

Hope died too. She lived for about three weeks after I wrote the last story. At first she seemed fine, as her sister Heidi did. She pranced around outside, excited to be in the spring sunshine. Then she stood still more than she pranced. Soon she stood hunched, her back curved upward and her eyes down. Eventually it became clear that her eyes saw nothing, that all her remaining energy was turned inward. Within a few days her life had run out like water down the drain, and she was just an awkward, stiff, thin corpse.

What are we supposed to pray for in this fallen world? Those saved from death will still die. The welcome rain that falls after a drought will turn to floods. The prayed-for marriage, job, or children will bring struggle and heartbreak. Often I feel my prayers for life and healing go unanswered; often I don't even want to pray. Is God like the doctor in an anecdote my family used to tell? Called to the bedside of a young mother in labor, he sat down, leaned back, lit his pipe, and said, "Well, let's just let nature take its course."

I think I know the source of my disappointment with God. I love creation so much that I forget about God except as its creator. Mostly I don't long for union with God whatever the cost; I long for a healed and perfect world, where babies of all species don't die and weather blesses instead of destroying. I hate to admit it, but I suspect that if I had that perfect world, I would turn to God less often than I do now.

So this world of death and distress is providing me with training in turning to God. Oh, but I don't like the training! I gather that once I have learned to hold God's creation more lightly, it will be restored to me perfected, in all its glory. Is it worth the cost? I have to accept that it is. I need to learn to live in the between time, like Lazarus, between new birth and inevitable death, between current imperfection and future perfection.

Again my daughter showed me the true life of faith in this world of death. She wrapped Hope in a knitted jacket and carried her gently around, even after she knew there was no—well, hope—of her living. She fed her what she could and warmed her when she could. Hope, like Lazarus, died, but she died loved. I'm not sure that is enough, but it is what I have been given.

Good shepherd, care for your flocks.
We slip so soon through the gates
and are gone.
May we find as we fall into darkness
the arms of the shepherd holding us,
and the voice of the shepherd calling us
to the green fields beyond the river.
Amen.

≡{ CHAPTER SIX }≡

April and August

The seed catalogues start arriving in January. While gloom and cold reign outside, I huddle before the wood stove and dream of the perfect vegetables pictured in them. I cover floor and table with successive editions of lists and garden layout diagrams. Every year I'm convinced that this year will be different. (Don't laugh, you gardeners. Admit you've thought it too.) This year I will keep better records and weed consistently; I will pinch back and thin and deadhead, painful though the process is. This year the weather will cooperate, and my life will not spring any interfering surprises on me.

I am still filled with this conviction, this dream of perfection, when April blows in. As soon as there is a break in the rain long enough for the soil to dry, my family and I work outside. Above us, returning cranes, creaking like rusty bedsprings, fly so high we can hardly see them. We till and weed and rake the garden plot. And there it is: a blank canvas waiting for its artwork, a blank page anticipating its literary masterpiece. We measure

31

rows with string and sow onions, potatoes, and lettuce. In a few weeks the warm-weather crops go in, and a gorgeous patchwork quilt of green covers our land. I rest on the cool grass and imagine the months ahead.

In the past, I grew tomato wrestlers that pinned their strangled cages to the mat of mulch beneath, but this year the tomatoes will embrace their supports like ballroom dancers. The onions, groomed and stately, will march up their rows like dignitaries, not like tipsy revelers reeling haphazardly over the property. The zucchinis will be self-controlled and produce no vulgar excess that we will have to abandon on neighbors' doorsteps in the middle of the night. I anticipate some gentle weeding and a pleasurable harvest. Since I'm dreaming, I even go so far as to imagine that my whole family will like what I grow and willingly eat it. It's a restful picture and one I delight in on the first sunny days of April.

Then August comes. My vegetables sprawl on the ground, exhausted by their own fertility and by the battle for earth, sun, and water. Around them the weeds, the annoying relatives of the plant world, park their jalopies and spread out picnics, letting their kids run wild no matter how I chase them with fork and hoe. Indoors, the fridge, counters, tables, and baskets are overflowing with produce that needs to be eaten or preserved fast, before it spoils and before more is ready to pick. The kitchen is steaming hot from the canner, but the garden, baking beneath the sun, is hotter still. The kids remain willing to dig potatoes—it's like a treasure hunt, they explain; you never know what you'll find—but we are all sick of searching for green beans and of finding boat-sized zucchinis moored under concealing leaves.

Eventually the green bean river stops flowing, and the onions and potatoes are all picked and stored. The herbs are dried, the sweet corn frozen, and the cucumber plants, having yielded salads and jars of pickles, compose themselves to rest. The tomatoes and peppers will keep going until the morning at the end of September when each leaf and blade of grass is outlined in frost. By evening, the plants will be brown mush; we gather the last green tomatoes to fry or ripen indoors. Soon the cranes will be heading south. All the shovelings of straw and manure from the goat barn will be strewn on the garden patch, the canner will be put away, and we will carry firewood from its piles under the maple tree to stack next to the stove. We too, worn out by the overwhelming fertility of creation, creep inside and rest.

I don't even think about the garden for a while, but eventually I take stock. I have to admit that the tomatoes did take over the garden, and we ended up composting more zucchinis than we should have. The weeds may not have won entirely, but they kept up their guerilla warfare till the last. My garden never, except for maybe a brief moment in May, looked like the pictures. But these realizations won't matter for long. I have a few months to—not forget, exactly, but allow the memories to soften before April comes around again.

How is it that I dare to dream every year of perfection sprouting from the hard shell of disappointments? I remember August, but if in April I believed my memories, I would never plant again. Somehow, I still make a garden, make friends, make resolutions, make one more attempt to conquer sin and despair, despite my lifetime of missing the mark. Somehow I still turn back to God's outstretched arms, after having turned away again and again. It must be that my renewal of determination has the same source as the power pushing from the seed. It's the undying force of Life itself. It is hope.

Dear Lord and provider of all we need,
thank you for the power of light,
the blessing of water,
and the humble mystery of dirt.

Thank you that within the hardest, driest seed
new life lies curled, ready to sprout,
without our having to do anything
but stand, hoe in hand, and marvel at your goodness.
Amen.

=={ C H A P T E R S E V E N }=

Consider the Dogs

I've had a few dogs over the years, but there are three that stand out in my mind: Mama Dog, Marshall, and Archie.

Mama Dog came into our yard to starve to death when my husband and I were living in Liberia. I saw her skeletal form collapsed on the edge of our property. I felt despair and even rage. One more West African tragedy I could do nothing about, I thought; one more harrowing evidence of human cruelty and the hostility of fallen nature. I wanted her to go away and die somewhere else.

She didn't. The next day she was still there, her head slightly raised when I came out the door. Again in a kind of fury—against the dog for making me feel this way and against myself for getting involved—I tossed some old bread toward her and went back inside. The next day she was marginally closer to the door; I didn't have to throw the food as far this time while saying, "I do NOT want a dog, you understand. Eat up and then take yourself off."

Within a week she was on the back porch, much restored and

seeming not just resigned to but delighted by my presence. She had probably never been deliberately fed before. The Liberians of our town didn't do anything with dogs except "chunk" rocks at them when they got too near. Most of the animals were wild, surly mutts, but this dog had no resentment. She seemed determined to live on our porch, so we gave her a name—Mama Dog, because she had obviously had puppies recently.

Around this time I bought a can labeled "Vienna Sausages." They were too nasty to eat, so I took a couple out to the porch for Mama Dog. She had never been given sausages before, even such bland ones as these. She looked at me in disbelief when I held one out to her—I couldn't possibly mean for her to eat it! Since she wouldn't take it, I laid it across her front paws. Even then she sat there long enough for us to go inside, get the camera, and take a picture of her staring in wonder at the glory of sausages. Eventually, once she was convinced she was allowed to, she ate them.

Mama Dog lived with us for a year. Every day she walked with me to the curriculum center where I worked and flopped down on the porch to wait. In the evening she followed me into the teacher training class I taught and curled up under the desk. Everyone in town knew where I was by seeing if the dog was outside or not. She tried once to come inside our house but never asked again after I said no. She barked at strangers, but if she had ever seen someone admitted to our house, she let him pass. She put on weight and filled out, but she was never pretty, with her bat ears, pointy nose, and inelegant caramel coloring. However, she was pretty enough for the local "lotharios," and soon we had puppies in a box on the porch. She was a good mother to them, although it seemed to pain her not to come with me to work.

When the puppies were old enough to take care of themselves, a distemper epidemic swept through town. There were dead dogs in the gutters of most streets. Mama Dog got sick and died within 36 hours. In her last hours, she lay on the porch, her home, stretched out on her side and gasping in agony. I could do nothing but impotently mourn and rage. I bent over her and touched her head; her last act was to wag her tail at me.

Marshall came almost twenty years later. He was a sheltie, rescued after five years of being chained outside with only occasional food or water. For months, he was too afraid to sit down in our presence. He never liked going outside much. Sudden movements or sounds made him cower. But he loved us. Once he came to believe that a day might hold something good, he would greet us at the bottom of the stairs any time one of us descended. It didn't matter if people had come down the stairs twenty times in the last hour, it was still an occasion of rejoicing for Marshall. His people had gone away and now they were back! The remainder of his life was sprinkled with delighted exclamation points. He had people! And food! And a couch that he was occasionally allowed to sit on! It was almost too much for him to bear sometimes; he would start barking as loudly as he could and have to be given a gentle squirt of the spray bottle.

Marshall was a musical genius. When our daughter played violin—when she even began to tune—Marshall would come running from wherever he was and stand stiff with anticipation. As she began her scales, he joined her in warming up. Aaarooo! Up and down the octaves—he took his art very seriously. Sometimes he would rumble and other times soar into falsetto. He achieved Baroque ornamentation on some notes—rooro-orooroo—and had a particularly effective vibrato in his upper register. We could see by his expression that he was lost in the music, although every now and then, when our laughter got too raucous, he would lose concentration and look over at us. My daughter took to practicing violin upstairs in her room, but he could still hear that first string being tuned and would sing with her from the bottom of the stairs. He was polite about all our other instruments, but none of them moved him like the violin.

Marshall died one spring on Holy Saturday. He had been weak and failing for some time. His attitude was never one of complaint but of apology that he couldn't wait at the bottom of the stairs or sing for us any longer. He too in his dying was more concerned with his love for us than his own pain.

And now we have Archie. He is another sheltie from the same rescue organization; he joined us in September. He was terrified of everything when we first got him. We had to leave his leash on even in the house so we could corner him when we needed to. But he desperately wanted to be loved, and now he will curl up with us on the furniture and heave a sigh of relief and satisfaction that he is somewhere safe with someone safe. He is under the computer desk as I'm typing this; when I get up he will follow me closely everywhere I go.

"Dog" has been a term of insult in almost every culture. There have certainly been dogs I didn't like. I've been threatened, bitten, and harassed by dogs. Dogs have fleas and unpleasant habits. I understand all of that. But Mama Dog, Marshall, and Archie, better than any treatise or homily, have illuminated for me the theological virtues of faith, hope, and love.

Faith to believe that, after a lifetime of abuse, something might be different, someone might be different; faith that past experience doesn't always limit future possibilities. They have had faith in me, a person who is often annoyed, impatient, and resistant to sentiment, and their faith has made me act more like the person they think I am.

Hope—surely hope is the defining characteristic of a happy dog. Every waking moment is spent in enthusiastic anticipation: Food?Food?Food?Food? Pat? Pat? WalkwalkwalkWALK? Only physical death quenches their hope for happiness, and even then, at the brink of death, they can be distracted from that great travail by one more hope—Pat? Pat?

And love. What have I, sinner that I am, done to deserve the love of such beautiful creatures? Love characterized by ongoing, unquestioning forgiveness, with no resentment, that delights simply in my presence. Love that forgets itself and only sees its object.

Lord of faithfulness and humility,
thank you for companionship
found in an unfamiliar form.
Is this friendship a remnant of Eden,
a foreshadowing of your coming kingdom?
Let me prepare for the new heavens and new earth
by becoming more like my dogs
in faith, hope, and love.
Amen.

Part Two

OURSELVES

CHAPTER EIGHT

The Shared Life

I'm not really a Luddite. I am, after all, typing this on a computer. When my husband buys me a kitchen appliance such as a toaster or a rice cooker, I do use it. I'm also not Amish and have never wanted to be, but I appreciate how the Amish weigh technology to determine if its effect on their community will be positive or negative. I like how their decision whether to use it is based on the community, not the technology. Cars, for example, can be ridden in if needed but generally aren't used, because too much mobility draws people away from each other. People who sit and stare at television screens are not talking to their friends and families or working outdoors in nature, so the Amish don't have TV. Instead, they have a community.

People seem to agree that community is something we all need. At least it's one of those feel-good words that get added to advertisements and political rhetoric to evoke an unthinking positive response. Although many of us spend our days in cars staring at roads and in cubicles staring at screens, we still have the idea that community—whatever the word means—is a human requirement and that we need to get it somehow. But what is it, and how can we make one or find one?

According to one dictionary, community is a group of people living in the same place and sharing a feeling of fellowship with others as a result of common attitudes, interests, and goals. Community involves physical proximity. It involves bodies. It involves land and shared space—not just cyberspace but rooms and parks and churches. It involves shared experiences, good and bad, that you can't edit or delete. In community, people sit down to eat together and get up to work together; they don't gulp fast food while faxing a memo. Genuine community grows, with all the painful and awkward stages of any human growth. Community isn't a website, despite the term "online community." It is also not something that can be constructed by developers, planners, or advertisers. It can't be bought. If we want to find, or make, a community, we have to do several things.

First, stay put. I'm just learning this one. I have finally begun to grow into a community after a lifetime of being a stranger. Yesterday in the grocery store, for instance, I was stopped and greeted by people from church, a student from my writing class, and a fellow master gardener who wanted to talk about vegetable judging at the upcoming county fair. I like this; I enjoy feeling that my life is entwined with the lives of so many people around me. Here is where I'll stay, unless God decides otherwise.

Second, stay slow. I always enjoyed the scene in Laura Ingalls Wilder's *Farmer Boy*, when Almanzo asks his father about using a new threshing machine. Threshing would go so much faster with it, Almanzo points out. But then, his father answers, what would he do with that time? He enjoyed winter afternoons in the barn with his son, threshing grain by hand.

We have added more and more labor- and time-saving devices to our lives over the last century, and we have less and less

time to do what we want. I'm not saying anything new; people
have made this point for decades, but I don't think we've heard
it yet. We are still being inundated with the newest, the latest,
the fastest—and somehow instead of getting more leisured, we
just have to run faster to keep up with our phones and computers and e-mail. Who has time for the slow growth of relationships with people and places?

Third, stay simple. One of the disadvantages of living in one
house for many years is that things accumulate. When I moved
every few years, I appreciated the discipline of having to get
everything I owned into a few footlockers or at best a U-Haul.
My challenge now is to keep that simplicity. It's amazing how
much time is devoted to taking care of stuff. I wash it, dust it,
move it, fix it, stack it, store it, get rid of it, and then buy more of
it—that's not how I want to live. I want to have time for people
and places, not stuff.

Fourth, stay connected; stay vulnerable. And here's where it
gets hard, at least for me. I may write about community, but I
don't really want to be connected and vulnerable. Sure, I like
people—some people—and love my family and a few friends.
But I'm the one who, as a missionary to the Kyrgyz, had the
unbidden thought that Kyrgyzstan would be a wonderful place
if only the people would leave. May God forgive me, but I did.

Real community is difficult. The "community" that is planned,
built, marketed, and sold is too easy. It's like buying a doll that
you can turn on and off instead of giving birth to and raising a
real baby. Community is messy and painful. Like every other human endeavor, it doesn't always work well in this between time. I
don't mean to sentimentalize: communities—Amish ones, too—
can be ingrown, vicious, invasive, and gossipy. Consequently,
growing up and leaving the community of one's birth is a popular American pastime, for what seem like good reasons. Even
healthy communities can be hard to keep balanced. I enjoy run-

ning into so many acquaintances in the grocery store, but I also get twinges of panic—am I entwined with my neighbors, or am I strangled by them? I have so many obligations now—to neighbors, friends, work, church, civic organizations—that the creative, relaxing, lonely anonymity of my earlier life has vanished. Days seem busier than they were, and schedule conflicts pile on top of each other. Is this a good thing? I don't know. What does a healthy community look like?

I have come to realize in the last few years that the training ground for healthy community is the church, specifically the Catholic Church. It understands who we are and how we have been made. The church community grows out of the deeper incarnational theology of our faith, which insists that both physical and spiritual realities reveal God's nature, because God is both physically and spiritually real.

Staying put: the Catholic parish system recognizes the importance of place. Ideally, it counteracts the American consumer mentality that can arise from the congregational model of church by uniting us with people of all types just because we live in the same spot. We have common attitudes, interests, and goals, as the definition says, but they are common because we have a shared relationship to God, not because we've sought out congenial people.

Staying slow: the liturgy sets the tempo for us, regardless of how jangled we are when we get to Mass. We are shaped by the deliberate repetition each week of words that have been said for centuries. Some churches offer drive-through communion, but the Catholic Church doesn't. We still have to be there and slow down, and that is a blessing.

Staying simple: while any individual in the church may struggle with the accumulation of stuff, the church itself, at its best, offers beautiful witness of the simple life and the joy of those saints who have embraced it. The church holds that it is good to lay up treasures in heaven, to invest in eternal things instead of stuff.

Staying connected and vulnerable: what can be more connected and vulnerable than the life of Jesus, who died for the sake of the world? Jesus *is* connection, the bridge between us and the Father. During his earthly incarnation and each day in the Mass, he offers us the ultimate union—the branch to the vine, the member to the body, the bride to her bridegroom.

True community must involve bodies because God took on human flesh; God did not just become a cyber-idea in e-space. Community means submitting ourselves to one another out of reverence for Christ. Community means eating together, celebrating the source and renewal of our life, both physical and spiritual, and our gratitude for it. Community must involve land because God made this earth for us to inhabit, and when the kingdom of heaven comes in its fullness, we will occupy the new heavens and the new earth—presumably with dirt and rocks and trees and animals, not just clouds and harps. Community as I'm describing it here is the result of the two great commandments: to love God and to love our neighbor. And it seems to me that any technology, worldview, or lifestyle that gets in the way of it is just not worth it.

Break down my walls, Lord,
and build a bridge
to span the gap between me
and the community of your body.
I must also ask
for the courage to cross.
Amen.

CHAPTER NINE

Should Christians Covet Poverty?

Some American Christians sentimentalize poverty. They long for it as a simpler, more holy lifestyle. They read accounts of praise-filled believers in far countries who barely have enough to eat or a roof over their heads, and they wonder if maybe poverty is a helpful or even necessary condition for the Christian life. Jesus did tell the rich young ruler to give away everything and follow him. If we're not doing that, maybe we're not in a right relationship with God. Should we covet poverty?

Well, let's consider what poverty really is. I don't mean income below the poverty line, because that varies from place to place. I also don't mean voluntary simplicity, which is another topic entirely. My working definition of poverty is *"want imposed by habit and circumstance, resulting in needs that cannot be met."*

I've seen poverty, and I didn't like it much. Let me share a few glimpses with you.

A grandmother, an abandoned wife, and three hollow-eyed children living in one room, with no food and only a threadbare rug and a few mats to protect them from the minus-twenty cold outside—this is one view of poverty. I don't covet this lifestyle. Neither do the people living in it.

Families around the world generally don't benefit from poverty. I knew a beautiful little child in Liberia who only answered to "Girl." She didn't know her name. Children there aren't expected to live, so parents just call them "girl" and "boy" until they're past the age of greatest risk. That way parents insulate themselves from caring too much.

I've cared for young people in the same country who died from preventable illnesses, whose relatives just shrugged in sad bafflement when they told me of the death.

I asked a poor woman I knew about her two-year-old daughter. "She hasn't walked in three days," my friend said. I had some cases of powdered infant formula that had been left by a medical team. I gave them to her, just as something healthy for the child. The next day my friend told me in delight that her daughter was up and walking again. It turned out that the formula was the only food the girl had had that week.

Poverty is not only physical deprivation; it's corrosive to the spirit as well. Once, a house caught fire in a Kyrgyz village. Along with everyone else, an American woman who was visiting ran out to look. "Shouldn't we do something to help?" she asked. Her host spat on the ground and said, "No, it serves him right. He was the richest man in the village. Let his house burn."

From resentment to covetousness is a short step. During my years in poor neighborhoods, here and overseas, I've been robbed several times. Poor children playing with my kids often couldn't concentrate on the toys they were invited to share.

They only wanted to have them for themselves, to steal them, even if that meant they could never play openly with them again. They didn't expect ever to get toys by any other means.

I had a Kyrgyz friend who began to ask me for things every time she came over to my house. I gave happily; I gave pragmatically; then I gave resentfully. I had become an object, a resource, to her. I was no longer a friend and a person. Finally, I demanded, "Do you think I'm a store? You used to come over to visit me; now you're just going through my things looking for what you want next."

What a terrible thing to say. Even though I was living simply by Western standards, I had a lot more than she did. But sadly, my generosity, in that and many other cases, didn't always build a relationship but instead destroyed it. I learned not to give as frequently as I wanted to. There were many people I would have been happy to help over the long term. But the money or things I gave engendered shame and resentment in them, and I never saw them again. People living in poverty, it seems, don't always respond well to blessings or know how to seek their own good—any more than we more well-off people do.

Poverty causes many to see others as resources to exploit. When I lived in Central Asia, the doorbell rang at least three times a day—I do not exaggerate—with people asking for money. The funniest may have been the woman who asked if I was a Christian. "I am too!" she declared, a remark that put me on my guard. (There were very few Christians, and we already knew them.) This woman hurled herself to her knees. "O Jesus!" she shouted. "O God! Help this American woman!" She made a fumbled gesture over her chest, then clasped her hands, closed her eyes, and began muttering. "You can get up," I said, torn between embarrassment and amusement. She did, saying, "Can you give me fifty dollars?" No, I said I wouldn't do that. "Twenty?" I began ushering her toward the tall, metal gate. "Ten?

Just something for bread?" I propelled her gently outside the gate and shut it behind her. As I did, I heard a companion whisper, "So, what did you get?" "Nothing!" she answered in disgust.

Despite our rosy view of it, poverty doesn't necessarily make Christians better people either. One Kyrgyz man approached my husband and told him he was a Christian. My husband said he was glad to hear it. "So now," said the new believer, "I want you to provide me with an income. Since I'm a Christian, I don't want to work anymore." It seemed that Christianity, for him, boiled down to an easy escape from a hard life, not the beginning of a right relationship with the God of Life.

Poverty didn't make these people saints. It wasn't a blessing to them. It ground them down. They lived meagerly in all ways, spiritually as well as physically.

But not all poor people are like this. I have been overwhelmed by the generosity of people Westerners would consider poor. There was the Liberian pastor who found me stranded at the side of the road as night was falling. He drove me far out of his way, late at night, while running short of gas, and wouldn't take a cent from me. "Americans have been kind to me before," he said. "I'm happy to return what I can." There were many people who brought out the last of their food in genuine delight that they had something to share with me. There was the Muslim family in Guinea who late at night welcomed my husband and me, complete strangers, and gently rolled their sleepy children out of bed so we would have a place to rest.

For several years, I lived in a rough neighborhood in downtown Indianapolis. My husband and I had three young children at the time. We weren't poor, but many people around us were. Two incidents stand out.

Once, my kids and I went for a walk. On our way home, they spied a White Castle and asked if we could get something for a treat. I hadn't brought my purse and only had a dollar or two in my pocket, but I said, "Sure, we can split a package of fries or something." Inside, as we stood in line, the three-year-old started asking for a hamburger. "Nope," I said, "we don't have enough money." The elderly man in the worn-out clothes standing behind us bought my children hamburgers. "It's all right," he said when I protested. "You happen not to have money just now, and I do."

Another time, I was shopping at a thrift store for a few winter clothes for my seven-year-old. The store didn't take checks, and though I had plenty in the bank, I had a limited amount of cash with me. We came out short, so I turned to put the gloves back. Once again, a man behind me in line—maybe homeless, probably struggling with mental illness—bought the gloves for my daughter. "I've known what it's like to be cold," he said. Though it shamed me, I could only accept, because he wanted so much to give.

It seems that sometimes poverty leads to covetousness, sometimes to generosity. Many poor people live in squalor, while others keep the little they have in spotless order. Some exploit friends for their own advantage, while some are extravagantly generous to strangers of different race, nationality, or religion. There are poor people who curse the ugliness of the world; there are also poor people who delight in the beauty of each day. So it isn't poverty that makes the difference here. What makes the difference?

Gratitude. I don't just mean gratitude toward people, although that's important. Gratitude is the expression of our right relationship with God. To learn gratitude, we have to know who we are and who God is. When we begin to know that, gratitude is the result. Once we know, really know, that everything we have is a gift from God, then what can we do but be thankful? An unredeemed understanding, on the other hand, sees everything as random occurrences or as the fruits of our own deserving. There's no need for gratitude in that worldview.

In some cases, it might be that poverty can help people to see who they are and who God is, to see reflected in their humble position before others their even humbler position before God. But not in all cases. All of the people I described above were certainly poor by our standards. Only some of them were grateful. Gratitude is not the result of poverty but a chosen response, as much within our control as any virtue or act of will is. The words and behavior of the man in downtown Indianapolis, the Liberian pastor, and the Guinean family reflect their awareness that they had been blessed and were happy they could pass those blessings on to others. Aside from the pastor, I don't know that any of those people were Christian; I know some were Muslim. But still they had the foundation of a relationship with God. They had some understanding of the first and great commandment and the second that's like it: they loved God with a grateful heart, and they loved their neighbor.

I began by asking if Christians should covet poverty. That was a trick question. Christians shouldn't covet anything, because covetousness is a sin. When we wealthy people long for poverty and complain that we'd be better Christians if we were poor, we're sinning. We aren't being grateful for what we have. We aren't displaying a right relationship to God or understanding his providence for us. We don't have to be in want to realize our position before God. God's gift of wisdom and enlightenment extends even to comfortable, insulated, slightly overweight people with too much stuff. It's nothing we earn or deserve by our economic standing.

So if you are wealthy—and chances are that you who are reading this are wealthy by world standards—give thanks for your wealth. If you become poor, voluntarily or involuntarily, give thanks for your poverty. In everything give thanks. Love God and your neighbor. Recognize your blessings and discover the freedom to give as extravagantly as you have received. Be awestruck by the beauty of creation and how utterly undeserving you are in the face of it.

My Lord and provider,
give me grace to hold the burdens of both wealth
and poverty lightly, in open hands.
May I acknowledge your generosity
by giving generously to others,
and may I bless others
as so many have blessed me.
Amen.

=[CHAPTER TEN]=

How the Whole Town Threw Us a Wedding

I t was hot and steamy, though surprisingly not raining at the moment. My thin dress clung to my skin. The air smelled of jungle, mildew, and iron-red dust. I could hear the rustling of people behind me and the occasional shout of pidgin English from the road outside the church. My knees were shaking, so I stiffened my legs and focused on the shattered eyeglass lens of the pastor in front of me. How did he see the world? I wondered. Was everything a kaleidoscope of lines and colors and shapes? That seemed appropriate. Our lives had been a crazy kaleidoscope ever since we arrived in Liberia nine months ago.

"Do you, Andrew," the pastor intoned in his rich West African voice—and then paused as he looked for the next line in the borrowed prayer book. The pause grew awkward.

"I do!" said my soon-to-be husband gamely.

"Wait! I'm coming!" Pastor Saidee scolded him, then found his place and continued through the marriage ceremony. He messed it up; we messed it up: one of our guests said afterward that ours was the funniest wedding she'd ever been to.

It had not always been funny getting to this point, though.

Andy and I met as Peace Corps volunteers in Liberia in 1985. We had six weeks together in training, with ninety other Americans and some wonderful Liberian trainers. We knew we liked each other right away, but we hardly had time to get to know each other in the midst of the mob. There's a photograph of us taken by a friend of ours (at least he was until that point) showing us sitting up in a tree in the dark of night, illuminated by a glaring flash. We had thought the tree was one place we could have a little privacy.

When training was done, we were assigned to different towns—he to Zwedru, I to Gbanga. They were not much more than 150 miles apart, but the one road that connected them was the consistency of oatmeal in the rainy season. It could take a week to travel the distance, and sometimes the road was impassable. There were no phones or postal service. We wrote letters to each other, adding on to them day by day until we heard of someone who was traveling to the other town and could take them. At least one of my letters was over forty pages long.

After six months we had had enough of this. We decided to get married, and the Peace Corps office, like a kindly Victorian father, approved our plans. I would move to Andy's town, where we would also have the wedding. Andy made arrangements for church, pastor, food, and everything else we needed.

Salwa Rizk, the wife of a Lebanese merchant in town, would make the cake, she told Andy—provided she could find eggs, sugar, kerosene (for her stove, not as a cake ingredient), and other essentials. We got gold rings made for us in the capital city. I made a skirt and commissioned a tailor to sew an embroidered blouse for a wedding outfit. We invited Peace Corps volunteers and other friends from around the country. We were ready.

A few days before the wedding, I traveled to Andy's town with the most precious of my belongings in a backpack. I left the backpack there with my wedding outfit, camera, prayer book, and the rings while Andy accompanied me back to Gbanga to help move my furniture. Travel at the height of rainy season was grueling. Again and again we got out to heave the little pickup truck through soupy mudholes. We finally got to Zwedru late at night, covered with mud and dust (somehow, Liberia manages to provide both at the same time), sweaty and exhausted, and looking forward to a bucket of water and some clean clothes.

We were not going to have them. Andy's house had been broken into while we were traveling. Everything was gone. We foolishly wandered through the house several times, as if our belongings would appear if we looked hard enough, but the cement floors and whitewashed walls just stared back. Andy owned nothing but the filthy jeans and shirt he was wearing. My wedding outfit and the rings were gone too. Fortunately, my furniture and dishes would help us make a new start, but "You'll put the wedding off?" asked a Liberian friend as he surveyed the emptiness with us.

No, we said; we'll get married in muddy jeans if necessary.

The dominoes of disaster continued to fall. A few days before, we had had clothes, a church, arrangements for a wedding cake, rings, a guest list—everything we needed. Now we had no clothes and no rings. The church Andy had booked cancelled because of a spat between local pastors. The regular heavy transport trucks got stuck in the mud, and no goods were arriving. There was neither sugar, eggs, flour, nor kerosene in the market for making a cake; there was no gasoline for people to travel with. And because the road was blocked by half-submerged trucks, the guests we had invited from other sites would not be able to make it even if they could find gasoline.

As so often happens, though, disaster opens the way for unexpected kindness. While Andy and I contemplated the ruin of our plans, people around us plunged happily into the wreckage to salvage what they could. In one of the greatest demonstrations of grace we've experienced, everything we needed was provided without our effort.

"You muh come wit me, ya," Sam Cooper beckoned. He had found a smith, he told us as we walked across town with him. The smith didn't have any gold, but he hammered out silver rings on a log and charged us five dollars each.

Madame Comfort Modjaka, the Ghanaian cook, came to the house as soon as she heard the story. "Eh, God!" she exclaimed. "It's too bad-oh!" She promised to cook the food for the reception; our first daughter's middle name is Comfort, after her. Two other people donated goats to be slaughtered.

The stores might be empty, but Salwa Rizk had somehow squirreled away the last ingredients in town and used a wood-fired clay oven instead of her kerosene one to make our wedding cake. The cake was a bit short, and a bit crooked, and it said "Happy Mariage" on top in red icing; it was nonetheless a beautiful wedding cake.

A Bengali engineer working in town gave Andy an embroidered Indian kurta (shirt) to wear, while a local tailor put aside his other orders and made a pair of pants. A Peace Corps volunteer lent me a white dress, which, because she happened to be wealthy back in the States, was a Laura Ashley creation. The Iranian wife of a Japanese UN worker had the same size feet as I did and lent me white shoes.

Finally the Baptist church said we could use their building for the wedding. Our Liberian friend Sam and our Peace Corps colleague Jamie—both of whom met tragedy a few months later—decorated the church with palm leaf arches and jungle flowers.

But we were still isolated from the outside world: the guests we had invited wouldn't come—we thought. We were wrong. People did everything they could to get there. One volunteer, braving hippos, crocodiles, and disease, forded a chest-high river with her wedding outfit on her head to get to us. The Liberian Peace Corps education director pulled strings and forced her way onto a tiny plane from the capital and got to the church with five minutes to spare.

It looked as if we were going to make it. Andy and I had been riding a roller coaster of stress and laughter during the preparations. As we headed into the church, we told another volunteer, "Look, Richard, if anything else goes wrong, just do something about it, okay?"

And there we were, under the arch of palm fronds and flowers, backed up by friends of eight nationalities, Hindu, Buddhist, Sikh, Muslim, Christian, and animist. I stared at Reverend Saidee's shattered eyeglass lens while my knees shook.

I mentioned that the ceremony was a bit rough. Reverend Saidee was more comfortable with exchanging cows than with the standard Western marriage rite and forgot that we had asked him to leave out the part about giving away the bride. (My father was 4,000 miles away.) There was an awkward pause after he said, "Who gives this woman?" Then Richard, mindful of our desperate plea, leaped up and shouted, "I give this woman!" to roars of laughter. The wedding picked up speed at that point, and by the time we got to the vows we were galloping. We went so fast that I forgot to promise for better, only for worse. Andy mentioned that as we went down the aisle. "Take what you can get!" I said.

We signed the palm-oil-stained marriage certificate; the illiterate registrar scrawled what might have been a signature in the corner. We were officially married. Our hands were shaken by all kinds of people in bright African outfits. When we reached the road, we were bundled into the Indian doctor's Land Rover to be driven to the reception in a cloud of dust and roaring engines. The doctor used his last ounce of gasoline chauffeuring us, escorted by Andy's Liberian coworkers on motorbikes, also burning the gas they had hoarded and blowing their horns every few feet.

We ate rice and goat meat with hot pepper in a crowded room, warmed by the affection shining from faces of every color. Outside the windows several dozen children stared in wonder, hoping that some leftovers might make it outside. They did; the rice and sauce were carefully doled out by a teenaged girl armed with a spoon for whacking any children who tried to finagle more than their share.

One of Andy's coworkers hushed the room after we had eaten. Voices died down and movement stilled. He made a speech; then he gave us a collection of over a hundred dollars to get us started as a married couple. People who had barely enough to survive on were giving us presents. Other gifts were proudly displayed on the table: a live chicken with its legs tied together, a wicker fish trap, some carved wooden wedding chains, a tie-dyed tablecloth with matching napkins, and a washboard.

We walked home, a married couple, laden with gifts, full of food, and exhausted from the busy day. It was almost dark; clouds were boiling up for the nightly downpour. The familiar smell of cooking rice and hot pepper came from the houses around us. Candles shining through open doorways lit the last few blocks to our bare house.

We had planned everything for the wedding, but our plans came to nothing. We lost control entirely of the situation. Through the gap created by our loss of control, a flood of kindness surged in. It's much better, I thought that evening, to have people who love you throw you a wedding than to do it all yourself. It's much better to have Someone who loves you throw you a life than to do it all yourself.

*It's funny, Lord, how I like to tell these stories
of disaster giving rise to happiness,
and yet when the next disaster occurs,
I forget the lesson you've taught me
and think I've been abandoned.
Thank you for the stories you give to remind us.
Never let us forget what you have done.
Amen.*

CHAPTER ELEVEN

A Brief Allegory of the Communion of Saints

From time to time, some Protestant Christians will express discomfort with the Catholic and Orthodox tradition of acknowledging the communion of saints. Someone will object to "praying to Mary" or "worshiping saints." Allow me to offer a parable in response.

Imagine a young woman who meets and falls in love with a man—let's call him Josh. They meet away from each other's homes, perhaps at work or at college. When they get engaged, Josh invites her home to get to know his family.

She's nervous, of course. Josh is a wonderful guy—far better than she deserves, she thinks. She's amazed that he picked her out of all the girls in the world. Her chief concern everywhere they go is to show Josh how much she loves him and is faithful to him alone.

They pull up to his family's house. A surprising number of people are silhouetted against the windows, and the front and back yards are full of clusters of conversationalists. As they get out of the car, she can hear people young and old talking about many things: other times, other places, science, philosophy, humor, etc. She feels slightly intimidated and grabs hold of Josh's hand. He smiles at her and brings her in to meet his mother and siblings.

The story is pretty familiar and predictable up to this point. Many of us have been through something like this. But here is where she has a choice—option A or option B.

Option A goes like this: she gets swept into a noisy crowd of people who all want to meet her; Josh is left behind. They hug her, ask her questions, laugh, get her a drink—they make her feel at home. She soon knows that not only has she found a husband, she's been adopted into a clan. Some of them, to be honest, seem a bit strange, but she reminds herself that she must seem strange to them. After an hour or so, she catches Josh's eye across the room and gives him a wave and a thumbs-up. He's delighted. Eventually, he will drive her home, and they can be alone to talk, but right now the music's starting up and she's being pulled into a dance.

Option B, on the other hand, looks this way: Josh brings his fiancée up to his mother, who is sitting on the sofa surrounded by smiling relatives. But instead of responding to his mother's greeting, the girl turns back to Josh and holds his hand more tightly. She does the same thing as aunts and uncles and cousins come to welcome her; she won't meet their eyes or talk to them. Though she doesn't go so far as to stick her fingers in her ears and chant, her posture suggests that she would if she could.

Soon she pulls Josh away to an isolated corner, leaving bewildered and slightly offended people behind her.

"What's the matter with you?" Josh asks. "Why won't you talk to my family? They're important to me, and they were excited about welcoming you."

"No way!" she declares. "I love you and only you. I'm not going to dilute our relationship or get distracted from you by spending any time with those other people. If our friends saw me talking to your cousins, they might think I was being unfaithful."

The allegory is obvious. The young woman is any Christian, Josh is Jesus, his mother is Mary, and his family represents the communion of saints, alive and dead. I've told the story this way to show how ungracious, at the very least, it is to Jesus and his family to ignore everyone but him. The girl is not going to marry everyone else in the clan, of course, but she will be a part of them forever. I'm sympathetic to the girl's impulse to be exclusively committed to her fiancé, but she needs to ask herself: How does it glorify him to be scornful of everyone else who loves him?

Many people who are uncomfortable with acknowledging the saints raise the point that saints are dead. It's one thing, they say, to visit, pray with, eat with, or complain to living people—they are happy to do all those things with their fellow (living) Christians. But conversation with dead people leaves them feeling squeamish. What are the mechanics of talking to dead people, anyway? Are we praying to them as if they were gods? Are we invoking their ectoplasm through a séance? Or are we just talking to the ceiling like forgetful old folks in nursing homes murmuring to lost loved ones? As a result of this confusion, many people react to the communion of saints like the young woman in the example above and determinedly ignore them.

I have no clue what the mechanics of "talking to the dead" are. In fact, I don't think you can talk to the dead. You can talk to persons who are alive in God, though. Samuel Wesley, a Protestant, wrote in "The Church's One Foundation" of the "mystic sweet communion" we have "with those whose rest is won." It's not a new idea that those who loved and served the body of Christ while they were here on earth still do so now (whatever "now" means once one has left the temporal world behind). The saints in glory are my in-laws, my new family, as are the Christians who are still in this world. I won't worship them, and I will only "pray" to them in the seventeenth-century usage of the word meaning to request attention of them.

I should acknowledge that there is one more option that our imaginary young woman has. She could make such close friends of Josh's mother or other relatives that she does end up neglecting him. That would result in a dysfunctional relationship, which is an ugly thing, literally or allegorically. There are wives who have done so with their husbands, and husbands with wives, and Christians who have done so with their Savior.

But let's not overcompensate and snub Jesus' family out of fear of idolatry. God sets the lonely in families, and our family of "happy ones and holy" is greater than we can imagine. So let's take our fingers out of our ears and make eye contact; let's plunge into the party. Rejoice, kick your shoes off, and join in the dance.

You who have gone before,
who wait to welcome us,
you martyrs and saints,
you quiet witnesses to the humble life,
mothers and fathers,
brothers and sisters,
pray for me to the Lord our God.
Amen.

CHAPTER TWELVE

Growing Old

More than a decade ago, when I was forty, I happened to glance into a mirror. It was a winter evening, and the room was lit by only a bare bulb. In the poor light, my face for the first time looked old. "I'm a severe old lady!" I thought, and thus began my mourning.

Mourning is definitely the right word for the denial, sadness, and endurance I experienced then—and still do now. I feel about my youth the same way I feel about someone who has died—the forgetfulness that buries the loss until something brings it to mind, the subsequent gut-wrenching sorrow, the resentment and desire to bargain...Why do I feel this way? I've thought of all the obvious reasons, but I'm not sure that they entirely explain my reaction to aging.

There's some vanity behind my mourning, of course. I was never beautiful, but I was nicer looking and in better shape thirty years ago than I am now. There's also the related loss of hope. Thirty years ago, if I didn't like how I looked, I could work out, get a different haircut, change my life, and somehow fix myself. But now no matter how hard I swim upstream, the current is still taking me downward. And every year I can't swim quite as powerfully.

There's the realization that all those things I planned to do one day are a lot less likely to get done. I may still learn another foreign language, but I don't think I'm going to climb Annapurna. And I'll ultimately be left behind by the young people who will—or at least might—do the things I no longer can.

Do I dread the kindly condescension that I'll receive if I live long enough? I already don't like the checkout clerk calling me sweetie and asking me if I have a senior discount. I may have some fear about my husband's and my ability to take care of ourselves, especially as I watch the nightfall of my mother's dementia. Perhaps I also sense my children's worry that we will grow old and leave them alone one day.

Yes, yes, I have answers—good, correct answers—for each of these. Old age is not coming as a surprise, after all. I've known since I was young that I would get old if I lived, and I've never tried to avoid or sugarcoat that fact. But those answers don't satisfy me, don't soften the long good-bye that I can see ahead as, with a painful squeeze of the heart, I notice that my husband's hair is graying or that my hands are getting wrinkled.

Certainly my sense of mourning is a result of sin; but do I mourn because of my own vanity and pride? That's a large part of it. But I also mourn because all people have mourned since sin and death entered the world. It could be that my feeling of "This isn't the way it's supposed to be!" is an accurate one. Aging would be a different thing if it wasn't for the Fall, I'm sure, and sometimes it intrigues me to speculate how glorious God's original plan for immortal life would have been—and then I mourn some more.

Well, I can't do anything about all the "ifs" and "buts." My only recourse is to deal with the life I have. I know that I'm healthy and capable, with a good family, a meaningful job that I can do for many more years, and surroundings of peace and plenty. I can thank God for stripping aside the accidents of my life and soul and helping me focus on their substance. I need to be grateful that God is enabling me to develop true faith, hope, and love and not just rely on the exuberance of youth. I should rejoice that God is introducing me to that perseverance that is so highly praised in Scripture. I can only lay down my life to God for loving me, a dying person. After all, I've been dying since I was born. God has not changed toward me since I've gotten older; I've changed toward myself.

These thoughts are all so true and wise and mature. I could write pages of philosophy and poetry and meditation—but I hate the whole process of aging with all my heart, and no philosophy or understanding mitigates that in the least.

How long, O Lord, before we are rescued
from the ravages of time
and can enter into eternity with you?
Still, not my will but yours be done.
Give me grace to accept my aging
and faith that I will wake from my final sleep
to see your face.
Amen.

CHAPTER THIRTEEN

A New Mission Field

H ave you ever thought you might have a calling to missions? I have a suggestion for you.

I won't try to convince you that this new field is more deserving or more desperate than a hundred others. All mission fields are important. People might get competitive about missions, but God calls different people to different jobs, and it could be that one of you might find your calling here.

"Here" is in rural and small-town America. But don't come to do vacation Bible school or build a picnic shelter or even start a church. Most small towns have a church and VBS, and we can build our own picnic shelter. What we need is a grocery store. A doctor's office. A hardware store. A co-op to package and sell locally grown produce. We need the necessities of life and meaningful employment in a place that feels like home.

My family and I live outside of a town of a thousand people in western Indiana. A hundred years ago our town still had a thousand people, but it also had a theater, a grocery store, a general store, two hotels, a high school, an elementary school, a grain terminal, a Carnegie library, and a hardware store. The last four remain. A few years ago the state tried to shut down the little library, but our petition drive was at least temporarily successful. The grain terminal will stay in business, I guess, and so will the elementary school—although several nearby have shut and some children now spend an hour each way on the bus. But our wonderful hardware store that smells of old wood and nails and oil and paint, with the window display of nineteenth-century implements and the mannequin legs sticking out of the claw-footed bathtub—it may close when the proprietor gets old.

That's what happened to the grocery store. It closed a few years ago when the owner needed to retire. No one replaced him, so the building is now sitting empty. I don't know whose fault it was that no one replaced him, but in any case we no longer have a grocery store. Now there's a gas station convenience store. It has twenty shelf-feet of chips and pretzels and five of macaroni and cheese packages and canned tuna, but it doesn't have a meat counter or fresh fruits and vegetables. We have to drive thirty minutes to get to a real grocery store. Oddly, the meat and vegetables in that "real" grocery store travel a whole lot farther to get there than we do—some from other hemispheres. The delivery trucks smoke through some of the most productive and fertile farmland in the world to deliver lettuces from California, grapes from Chile, and lamb from Australia. And the people around here who might grow lettuces or grapes or lamb are working part-time at the tanning salon or collecting food stamps.

Well, but be practical, you say. No one can make a living in a little town. It's true that the few businesses we have are mostly run by older people who, I presume, have their mortgages paid off and a Social Security check to help out. The cost of living is very much cheaper out here, as long as you don't have to drive an hour to shop and work; nonetheless, it would be hard to support a family by running a store in a town of a thousand people. That's why I say it's mission work.

Where are the wealthy churches willing to back a small business operator in a rural area as their mission project? How about those city churches with lots of professionals—could someone help to get grants for rural development, not just to keep open a necessary local store but to employ local people in local businesses? Mission work is not just church planting. Yes, rural people need a good church, but nowadays even good churches are filled with retirees; younger people, if they work at all, work an hour away, on late shifts and early shifts, and become disconnected from their community. Many young people don't work; it's cheaper to live on food stamps out here than in the cities, and frankly, people can do pretty much anything they want in their old trailers in the woods—meth labs are competing with farming in most Midwestern rural areas. So if you want grittiness and drama on your mission field, you can find it here: drug problems, broken families, teen pregnancies, hopeless lives— there is work for missionaries in these little towns and scope for active churches to get involved.

I know that running a doctor's office or grocery store in rural America isn't typically considered missions by many Christians. But if caring for people's daily needs is a means of mission work in Burkina Faso, why not here? Many of the needs are the same, and rural Americans, like Burkinabes, will respond to people who are humbly serving as the face and hands of Christ.

Picture this example. You open your grocery store. (We've got an empty building available for a good price.) You provide the basic necessities, and a few extras too. You begin to get a name around here for having the freshest produce and meat, because despite the labyrinth of government regulation, you've found a way to buy from local producers and sell to local consumers. In fact, some city folk disillusioned with produce from the other side of the world are driving out this way to visit your store.

If you do use our old grocery building, there's a room in the front with tables and chairs, where people used to play euchre and have community meetings. You line the room with display cases of local handicrafts—I can introduce you to some up-and-coming spinners, knitters, basket makers, carpenters, artists, and others. People can buy the crafts from you or pick up the craftsperson's business card after the community guild lunch or handicraft workshop or recipe exchange for seasonal produce. If you're creative with your insurance, you could even have a seasonal food-preserving kitchen, although maybe one of the churches would work with you on that.

You accept food stamps and WIC and have the time to chat with young parents about recipes and healthy cooking. You have some high-school interns working at the store who carry groceries for those who can't, or deliver groceries to people without cars. You can't pay them much, but you'll find every year that they ask you to write them recommendations for college and employment, and you're happy to help them out. As soon as the business is off the ground, you take on a young person as an apprentice—not just a minimum-wage slave, but someone you invest in. You'll have several apprentices over the years, because some will use their experience to go on to other things; but when you're old and ready to retire, there will be someone in place to keep the business going.

People will start asking you why you moved here: they'll probably say "way out here" or even "this dump." You'll have the perfect opportunity to start talking—slowly at first, because country people take a while to warm up. But after five or ten years, they'll be used to you. They know your family; you go to the Fourth of July parade and the Halloween cake walk with them. You don't idealize or condescend to them. You're their neighbor, and they'll share their lives with you in a way that most of them wouldn't with a pastor. People who have never seen a stable family—or a contented single person—will have you to look at, and a few young people will stay and farm their grandparents' land since they now have a market for their goods.

As gas prices get more prohibitive, these small towns will have a choice they haven't had in a hundred years: they could once again become true communities, with stores and schools and jobs and churches that people can walk to and neighbors who know and care about each other; or their residents can give up the struggle and move to the crowded, faceless cities, shop at 7-Eleven stores, and never know a plant or animal personally. You could be a part of that choice.

This mission assignment would be long-term, even lifelong, not a two-year trip with most of your time spent fund-raising and at conferences. You would be leaving behind the culture of the cities, the museums and private schools and stimulating ethnic mix you were used to. You would be taking on a job seen as low-brow and dead-end. You'd hear a lot of "You went to business school and now you're running a junky little grocery store?" from some of your educated city acquaintances. You'd hear a lot of "I can't wait to get away from all the losers in this place!" from some of your new neighbors. But even today, in our rich, spoiled society, there are Christians who are willing to sacrifice, to give up comforts, to go to strange places and serve alien people. Some Christians are even brave enough to do all that an hour down the road and forgo the glamor of newsletters filled with tropical photos and exotic stories.

And you know how it is—those who are called to the work don't deem it a sacrifice, ultimately. You might find, after a few years in the field, that you've never been happier. Sure, your rural route gets snowed in every winter, but your neighbor with the pit bull and the pickup comes at six in the morning to plow you out. Your children are learning patience and responsibility raising livestock, and nothing can beat harvesting your own garden every summer. The wood stove smells great in the winter; it's the magnet that draws your family into the living room of the big old house that cost a third of what an apartment would have cost you in Los Angeles. And best of all, you're a genuine Christian presence in a place that needs what you have to offer, living proof that to Christians like you community is more important than making money and getting ahead.

You may be asking why I don't do this myself. I'm not a business person; I'm no good with money. But I teach at a community college in a nearby rural town. I hope I'm providing encouragement and dignity to people who aren't much appreciated by the mainstream of American society, not to mention by American employers. My students and neighbors deserve a real community, with a doctor who knows them, and a grocery store, and a school, and things to do that are not contingent on the internal combustion engine. They deserve to see God's love in action in a way that Paul the tentmaker and James the advocate of charity would approve of.

And hey, I promise you we'll all shop at your store and even come in for the euchre games if the ice tea isn't too sweet.

Any takers?

God of all,
you have prepared work for us to do.
Show us our vocations and the places
where you want us to serve.
Enable us to see with your eyes
and serve with your hands,
however humble the work.
Amen.

CHAPTER FOURTEEN

The Seven Virtues

Quick! Name the seven virtues—the four cardinal virtues and the three theological virtues.

Did you have a hard time? It's funny (or maybe not) that many of us can name the seven deadly sins but have no idea what these seven virtues are. It seems that sins are still objective, nameable things, especially the deadly ones; postmodern people can still find some wisdom in identifying conditions of the heart that lead to wrong action and lack of action. Or maybe sins are just more familiar to us.

The *Catechism of the Catholic Church* defines virtue as "an habitual and firm disposition to do the good. It allows people not only to perform good acts, but to give the best of themselves. Virtuous people tend toward the good with all their sensory and spiritual powers; they pursue the good and choose it in concrete actions." The Catechism goes on to quote St. Gregory of Nyssa, reminding us that "the goal of a virtuous life is to become like God" (CCC 1803).

So according to the Catechism, virtue is more a disposition than an action, though it leads to action; it is what we are as well as what we do. It is the ground from which all the fruits of our lives grow. It is the habit of goodness. Virtue doesn't just buff us up to make us more attractive; it enables us to act with generosity and integrity to give the best of ourselves to others. Its goal is Christlikeness.

These foundational virtues lead to right action, but I think that many people in this generation have forgotten them partly because "virtue" has become a quaint, stiff, slightly embarrassing word that denotes virginity and connotes librarians; and "goodness" is seen as either a pink cloud of niceness and tolerance or Randian self-fulfillment at all costs. In any case, virtue is no longer seen as an objective standard one can train for.

But let's buck the trend and consider first the four cardinal virtues.

The Cardinal Virtues

The word "cardinal" comes from the Latin root for hinge, hence the pivot on which all other things turn. These virtues are pivotal to our actions and understanding. That there are four of them reminds us that any virtue, even (especially) our favorite one, can be distorted into a vice when it's not kept in balance with all the others.

The cardinal virtues are also called human or universal virtues because they are considered natural to all humankind—not because they are regularly achieved but because they are widely accepted throughout time and space as admirable human qualities. For thousands of years people have thought that one of the reasons we exist is to develop virtue. Whether developing virtue provided one with immortal glory or aligned one with the gods or God, generations have seen life as the battleground of character—not, as we do now, as the playground of whim.

An acknowledgment of universal virtues presumes a realistic view of the world. The ancient philosophers, church fathers and mothers, and great souls of all times and places focused on training in virtue because they knew that they had to prepare to live in a world of suffering, temptation, and imbalance. Confucius, Aristotle, Marcus Aurelius, St. Francis de Sales, and Gandhi all understood this.

Remembering and applying the wisdom of tradition rather than trying to reinvent wisdom every generation is an act of humility on our part. Like all elements of Christian tradition, the cardinal virtues serve as a check or guidepost to keep us from veering off the narrow path after the enthusiasms of our own age. They also give us a vocabulary to talk about an essential but neglected part of human history and human character. It's a vocabulary that needs to be retaught, I think. The names of many virtues have fallen out of common use, which makes me wonder whether the virtues they represent are equally unfamiliar.

So what are the four cardinal virtues?

Prudence. The word is another illustration of the degradation of the language of virtue. A "prude," in common usage, is a coward unwilling to embrace life fully, a snooty puritan condemning other people's fun. Even those who use "prudence" in a positive way strip the word of most of its robustness. Prudence is not just the careful, almost miserly, meting out of money, time, and self, as the word often suggests today. Prudence is "right reason in action," according to St. Thomas Aquinas. It is the practical wisdom that forms and guides our conscience and our ability to make choices. It is sometimes described as the charioteer of the virtues in that it directs and reins in our other impulses. It is, if I may use a probably inaccurate metaphor, the gear that connects the engine of our moral judgment with the wheels of our actions. Without prudence, we would neither recognize the right nor choose to do it. We train our children in prudence before letting them get behind the wheel of a car or go to school, work, or social gatherings without us.

Justice. Justice is the only one of these four words that retains some of the richness of its original meaning. Justice, however, is not simply sentencing evildoers or instituting fair laws. Justice is the virtue that gives everything its due. The just person treats creation, other people, and God as they should be treated, according to their natures and their rights. Justice cares for the poor and weak, upholds laws, respects human dignity, and shows honor to those in authority. It implies self-knowledge and an ability to understand one's place in the universe.

Fortitude. What does that even mean? The word is never used in conversation these days. Its closest synonyms are courage, strength, and steadfastness. Fortitude faces fear and death unflinchingly. It perseveres and remains constant against all trials. All people admire fortitude, even if they don't know the word. C. S. Lewis, in *The Screwtape Letters*, saw fortitude, or courage as he called it, as the foundation of all human goodness: "Courage is not simply one of the virtues but the form of every virtue at the testing point, which means at the point of highest reality." He explained that any virtue—prudence, justice, kindness, generosity, and so on—that buckles in the face of threat or persecution is no virtue at all.

Temperance. This is probably the most degraded word—and virtue—of this list. At its best nowadays, temperance means abstaining from alcoholic beverages; at its worst it conjures up the comical picture of indignant Victorian matrons waving placards and smashing storefronts. Even more than prudence, temperance is seen as the stingy denial of fun by narrow, frightened people. This is the opposite of the truth. According to the Catechism, temperance "moderates the attractions of the pleasures and provides balance in the use of created goods"; it "keeps desires within the limits of what is honorable" (CCC 1809). Contrary to what most would think, temperance, or the moderation of desires, is essential to fun. Rules and taking turns permit a game to be enjoyed. An evening with friends is more pleasant without waking up on the bathroom floor afterward. That's not the common perception, however. Justice and fortitude may still be admired nowadays, and prudence—or at least cleverness—may be accorded some respect, but temperance is absolutely at odds with the deepest assumptions of our culture. The practice of temperance would take from the advertising industry its most potent tools: "More! Now! Quick! Go for all the gusto you can get!" It would undermine the economic imperative of maximizing profit. It would put an end to unsustainable exploitation of natural and human resources. It would challenge the casual acceptance of lust, avarice, and gluttony that is such an integral part of our society.

We Christians can't stop here, with just the cardinal virtues, though. We have to have the right motivations to be truly virtuous. As Christians, we are warned against virtue motivated by legalism or competitive superiority. For us the reason to be virtuous is not to lord it over others less virtuous than we are. It is not even to console ourselves, in a bleak, stoic way, that even if everything around us is in ruins, we at least are true to ourselves. The right motivation to be virtuous, as well as the antidote to legalism, pride, and despair, is provided by the three theological virtues: faith, hope, and love.

THE THEOLOGICAL VIRTUES

The theological virtues of faith, hope, and love, or charity, unlike the human, or cardinal, virtues, are not universally recognized or admired. We don't see them as such in Stoicism, Epicureanism, Confucianism, or Taoism, for example, although we can find prudence, justice, fortitude, and temperance. In fact, a Stoic would think that faith in heaven or divine intervention was weakness and foolishness, and that true virtue was achieved by doing good without hope of it making any difference to the world.

Faith, hope, and love are not universally acclaimed because they are founded on the nature of the Triune God. They are absurd and pointless if you remove God—as absurd as the shower curtains for sale nowadays that say "Faith" in curly letters or the dish towels with "Hope" embroidered on them. Faith in what? Hope for what? Faith and hope without God are not virtuous; they are a naive optimism, a blind effort to "feel" nicely faithful and hopeful without any foundation.

Sacrificial love is equally pointless without God. It's true that through common grace, we are often blessed to receive love from people who come from a belief system that does not recognize it as a virtue. Some of the greatest acts of sacrificial love I've witnessed were performed by Muslims or followers of traditional religions; some of the most appalling offenses of greed and pride I've experienced were done by Christians. I'm not saying that the practice of the theological virtues is limited to Christians, just that faith, hope, and love are best recognized and appreciated by those who, consciously or unconsciously, are growing in the likeness of the Holy Trinity, in whom love finds its perfect expression.

Faith. Through faith, we believe in God. Through faith, we know, at least to some degree, God's nature, our nature, and what is required of us. Because of this knowledge, we can listen to our consciences, honor God and creation rightly, face difficulties with courage, and moderate our desires. So faith is a gift that underlies and enables the human virtues, but it also is a habit that requires action from us. It is inextricably united to good works as we obey God and begin to live the new life that God is pouring into us. It is the reason to share the good news of God's love with everyone, and to share it calmly and cheerfully, because we trust God's sovereignty and his care for all of us. Faith doesn't need human reward or praise or to see immediate results. Faith is peace and direction in the midst of the tumultuous world, a rock in the storm.

Hope. Hope, like faith, takes us out of ourselves. It reassures us that what we see around us is not everything, that time and death are not the ultimate boundaries. It teaches us a proper distrust of our own capabilities and a joyful humility in expecting something better than we can imagine. Hope is the foundation of joy. Hope is a gift of grace, but fortitude is required to hold on to hope in the midst of the darkness of this life. Because of hope we prepare for Christ's coming and the Day of Judgment— the hopeful person keeps oil in her lamp even when it seems a waste to do so. Hope is a beacon to a despairing world.

Love. Life and this book are too short to deal with all the meanings of this word. I'd rather say charity, but that word has also become degraded and nowadays often means exactly the opposite of what Paul describes in 1 Corinthians 13. Paul points out that the greatest of the theological virtues is this love that he is talking about. One day, we will see God face to face and we will no longer need faith; our desires for God, heaven, peace, and justice will be satisfied and we will no longer need hope; but on that day we will experience the fullness of love. Love is the opposite of the rock-hard unity of loneliness; it is relationship and community. It is the reason we were created and our reason to create in turn. Love is the only thing we can give back to God as our free gift; it turns us from slaves into children. The theological virtues end with love because, as St. Augustine says, "Love is the fulfillment of all our works. There is the goal; that is why we run: we run toward it, and once we reach it, in it we shall find rest."

It's hard writing about the virtues because they are both gifts we receive and actions we do. "Virtue" means an inherent quality, such as the virtue of iron being its strength, but it also means specific deeds of goodness and the training to make them possible. I think all meanings are important, and it's a challenge to keep them in mind at the same time. Our response to a call to virtue is equally complicated. We can't achieve or merit a gift, only accept it, but we can and must act in order to train ourselves into the habit of goodness. The balance between the gift and the action, being and doing, grace and works, is tricky and an appropriate subject for much prayer.

Although the human, cardinal, virtues are admired and taught by people who don't know God, that doesn't mean that they exist distinct from God—how could they? Nothing exists without God's grace; I could no more be brave or temper my appetites without God's grace than I could fly. All virtue, human or theological, stems from God's grace. I don't offer this meditation on the virtues as a self-help course. I offer it as an opportunity to praise and serve God according to the nature he gave us and the life he calls us to.

Finally, brethren, whatsoever things are true, whatsoever things are honorable, whatsoever things are just, whatsoever things are pure, whatsoever things are lovely, whatsoever things are of good report; if there be any virtue, and if there be any praise, think on these things. (**PHILIPPIANS 4:8**)

Part Three

GOD

=⟨ CHAPTER FIFTEEN ⟩=

The Journey

For some years, I attended evangelical churches. There was much good about them. They were great at pointing out that in ourselves we are dead in our sins. They preached loud and clear that the Christian life is not a self-help program. Any program that's offered as a substitute to being born again into the new life of Christ is a highway to hell. I agree.

I now want to take up the Christian life at Chapter Two. Chapter Two is that part of the Christian life that comes as we are born again into union with Jesus. It's the life that we live once we've staggered out of the tomb and begun struggling with our winding sheets. It can be a pretty long chapter. Most of us are not like the thief on the cross, whose literal and spiritual death and rebirth happened in the course of an afternoon. Most of us are going to live for years being remade into the image of Christ. We are going to strive for "a long obedience in the same direction." (I love that phrase, although it was Nietzsche who first said it.) Infused with our new life, we are going to have to work—to train and exercise and perform acts of goodness.

Yes, I know. I've been told many times by evangelical Christians that grace is all that is necessary to the Christian life. In a way that's true. Our resurrection from sin is grace, pure and simple, radical, appalling grace. But many of the Christians I knew stopped there. They said nothing substantial about the life we were to lead as resurrected Christians.

As a consequence, I spent years with nothing to do. I felt that I had been issued a ticket to Salvation and now I was supposed to sit on the platform and wait for the train. Oh, I could read a bit, and there were some fellow passengers to chat with, but it was an odd, in-between life nonetheless. I was marking time between the two important realities of the spiritual life: becoming a Christian (receiving the ticket) and going to heaven (getting on the train.) And there was no plan that I could see for the long years on the platform.

I wondered: could I walk ahead down the tracks for a bit? No, church people told me, I might miss the train, and besides, I'd never get to Salvation by my own efforts, so there was no point trying. Could I go do some other things in the town I'd left until the train came? No, stay with your fellow travelers and stop thinking that there's anything you can DO.

Well, I'd ask, what's Salvation like, anyhow? Is there any way I can prepare myself? Some exercises, maybe, or a course of study? The answer always seemed to be "Sit there and read your Bible." But I've **read** it! "Then read it again! And wait for the train. Oh, and whatever you do, don't lose your ticket."

I was bored. Bored to the point of falling off the platform in a stupor and landing on the rails. One more Bible study video course did nothing for me. One more women's prayer group, pleasant though it was, failed to bring light to my gray existence. The sermon series, the parenting series, all the programs that were (ironically) offered by the churches that scorned any effort to grow in virtue became about as life-changing as the billboards on the train platform. Is this all there is? I had thought that the Christian life was hard and challenging and important and occasionally (dare I say it?) fun. But it was just a safe, dull, dimly-lit waiting area. If this was the kingdom of heaven, then maybe Talking Heads was right: heaven is a place where nothing ever happens.

I don't want to blame any particular church or denomination for my doldrums. I wouldn't be surprised to find that other people in the church I attended at that time were leading exciting, growth-filled lives while I was just sitting around. But I am going to ask this question again: Isn't the Christian life supposed to be hard and challenging and important and, occasionally, fun? Were *The Narnia Chronicles*, the lives of the saints, *The Divine Comedy*, and *Pilgrim's Progress* all lies?

Part of the reason for the exaggerated passivity of some Christians is an extreme attitude about the relationship between our own sinfulness and God's grace. Because we can do nothing toward our own salvation, these extremists counsel, we should do nothing at all, even after being saved. All healthy, outgoing activities, like fasting, pilgrimage, or acts of mercy, they would immediately quash, because in doing those things we might mistakenly think we can impress or sway God. I've heard and read a lot of that and found it baffling and discouraging. Welcome to Christianity. Here's your seat. Don't move. Blah.

Well, I *don't* want to be driven by wretched urgency. I strive to avoid the sort of pride that assumes that God can't get the world saved without my input. But I still want to do something with my life. I want to begin the eternal journey of obeying what Jesus commands, to begin being perfect. Not in order to be perfect in the abstract, but to be like him, and to be with him.

I want to be prepared—for life with God, for heaven, for the Judgment whenever it comes. I am delighted that I can trust in

God's mercy. Now I want to do something in response.

A scene from *Anne of the Island*, the third of the *Anne of Green Gables* books by L. M. Montgomery, has stuck with me for years. Anne is talking with Ruby, a dying schoolmate, who says, "I'm not afraid but that I'll go to heaven, Anne. I'm a church member. But—it'll be all so different...Heaven must be very beautiful, of course, the Bible says so—but, Anne, *it won't be what I've been used to.*" And Anne makes a resolve. "It must not be with her as with poor butterfly Ruby. When she came to the end of one life it must not be to face the next with the shrinking terror of something wholly different—something for which accustomed thought and ideal and aspiration had unfitted her...The life of heaven must be begun here on earth."

I'm reminded of when I was preparing to go overseas with the Peace Corps. Many of us volunteers did lots of preparation. We bought practical gear, read books, worked out, took a first aid class, talked to people who had lived where we were going, got our finances in order—we worked hard. None of our work made our departure date come any sooner, of course, but it did have two benefits. First, it gave us a purpose and a joy while we were waiting; second, it prepared us for the new life we were going to face. In fact, in a small way we began living the new life even before it had entirely arrived. Other volunteers did no work in advance but only threw some things in a bag the day before they left. Most of them didn't stick it out. Most of the prepared ones did.

Or if you prefer a scriptural illustration to a personal one, think of Cornelius in Acts 10. He did not yet have in its complete form the faith that comes by hearing. God graciously sent Peter to tell him the Good News and to baptize him. But Cornelius is described, even before Peter arrived, as "a devout man who feared God with all his household, gave alms liberally to the people, and prayed constantly to God." He was beginning to live the life of God. And God's messenger told him, "Your prayers and your alms have ascended as a memorial before God." His works didn't save him and were no substitute for grace and the Good News, but they were pleasing to God, and in doing them Cornelius began down the path that Grace had laid for him.

It's true that sometimes we need to be reminded about "being," not "doing." But that isn't the only imperative of the Christian life. It can't always be evidence of weak faith or overweening pride to "do." Consider the parable of the talents recounted in Matthew 25:14–30. Let's face it: the first two servants *did* something with what they were given. They weren't earning their position as servants, because they were already members of the Master's household. But he had left them alone for a long time—had left them in a between time, between joining the household and receiving their reward. They didn't just sit around and talk about their unworthiness to work and therefore, indirectly, the Master's unworthiness to be worked for. They worked with what they had been given, in order to achieve something for their Master. The third servant, on the other hand, resented the supposed arbitrary nature of the Master and buried his money. He did nothing. And his reward was nothing.

I know God needs nothing from me. I love Milton's "On His Blindness," and I'll stand and wait if that's what God requires. But while I'm waiting I want to prepare myself for the place I'm going. I want something hard and challenging and important, and fun. I want training: *askesis* or asceticism.

Asceticism is the training of the Christian athlete for the Christian life, now and in eternity. If we haven't tossed out all Christian tradition, we can see that the last two thousand years have provided us with a wealth of wisdom about how—and how not—to practice *askesis*. Asceticism doesn't just mean hair shirts and all that goes with them. It is part of my daily life of faith in the Catholic Church: kneeling, fasting, confession, prayer, and submission to the guidance of the church, which insists that I not only fast but feast. I am beginning to find that the ascetic disciplines are hard, challenging, important, and, oddly, fun.

I'm not the first to be saying any of these things—which is good, because I have no intention of being original. Richard Foster, St. Teresa of Avila, St. Benedict, Brother Lawrence, St. Isaac of Syria, John Bunyan, Mother Teresa—all of them could say it better than I, in life as well as in words. But I will add my voice to the chorus, in homage to some of the ascetic disciplines outlined by St. Benedict in his *Rule*: humility, obedience, silence, chastity, prayer, work, stability, poverty, and hospitality.

I can't say much about how to practice these disciplines, since I am a neophyte myself. I can, I hope, offer encouragement to other Christians to consider them—to you Christians who are tired of sitting on the platform, who have always secretly hoped that there would be dragons to fight, quests to pursue, journeys to struggle through, and acts of love and mercy to perform— you who hope to hear "Well done, good and faithful servant!" when the Master returns.

There is work for Christians to do, and there are time-honored means of training for it. We can't just sit on the platform waiting for our train to come in. In fact, let me let you in on a secret. There is no platform. You're already on your journey. We all are. The question is just where you're going and how prepared you'll be when you get there. Pack well. Count the cost. As long as it is day, we must do God's work; night is coming, when no one can work.

Guide me on my journey, Lord.
I know I have to set out,
but I don't know the way.
Strengthen me for the road
and keep me faithful to the end.
Amen.

≡[CHAPTER SIXTEEN]≡

Free Fall

G rowing in faith is a dangerous proposition. It's been compared to leaping off a cliff: I can't see where I'm going, and I have to trust the results of my choice to someone or something beyond me.

Jesus more commonly talks about dying, especially in terms of dying as a sacrifice. "He who does not take up his cross and follow me is not worthy of me." He also said, "Unless a grain of wheat falls into the earth and dies, it remains alone; but if it dies, it bears much fruit. He who loves his life loses it, and he who hates his life in this world will keep it for eternal life."

Most of us are not going to die for our faith in a literal way, but we do have to face this leap. As we grow into the image and the likeness of God, we can't hold on to the railing or grab a parachute—we can't keep anything of what we were. We can't have "Christianity plus," to paraphrase C. S. Lewis—not Christianity plus social action, or Christianity plus conservative politics, or Christianity plus my opinion about homosexuality or women or wealth. All of it has to go. God will not be used as a stamp of affirmation for our opinions.

For example, maybe I've generally thought that being a nice person just means being tolerant of others' differences. Maybe I've always believed that Christians are more properly associated with the political left, or the political right, with socialism or capitalism. I have to sacrifice these opinions on God's altar. Even when my original opinions are actually right, are actually aligned with God's understanding, I still have to give them up—because they are based on my own righteousness, not God's. When we take the leap and drop into free fall, we can't be weighed down with all our baggage.

This is scary. How is this faith I'm talking about any different from the brainwashing of Jim Jones' followers in Guyana? They also were told to leap, to scrap their own ideas of right and wrong, to give up their ownership of themselves, to expect to have their own beliefs and habits overturned in every particular. And yet we would all agree that the mass suicide at Jonestown was wrong, was evil on a cosmic scale, and that the people involved in it were tragically deluded. Many of the people who followed Hitler also put to death their own sense of right and wrong, which seems to be what I'm recommending here, and they were led into unimaginable atrocities.

So what is the difference between the leap that Jesus asks of us and the one Jim Jones or Hitler asked of their followers? Some people—many people, I think—say that the difference rests in us. We have to be smarter than the victims of these cults. We have to weigh claims more carefully, trust less easily, hold back on our impulses to belong and follow, measure everything against what we think is right.

But I don't think that we should hold back from trusting and commitment, and the difference between cultists and Christians doesn't rest in our discernment or our moral strength. Only one thing protects us from the powers of darkness. Only one thing stands as the difference between true faith and perverted cultism. That one thing isn't our moral discernment, or our correct worldview, or our sturdy conscience.

That one thing, in fact, isn't a thing but a person. The difference is Jesus himself. If Jim Jones or Hitler asks us to leap off a cliff, he won't be standing there ready to catch us. God will. It's not the leap that's right or wrong; it's who is asking for it. We don't become better Christians by being more cautious but by knowing whom to trust.

For decades now I've been asked daily to leap. I've been asked to swallow and even forgive injustice to myself and others, though every cell in my body screams that it's wrong. I've been asked to give up my own ideas about what is nice, and loving, and proper, and to start wielding a two-edged sword, which really doesn't make me popular with anyone. All this effort and sacrifice, and how do I know I'm right? I stand on the cliff top and look into the unknown world beneath me, and my stomach clenches. Maybe I should just stay here, hanging on to my own jumble of convictions and individualism. But if I do, then I'll never enter the kingdom of God.

This is the great challenge of the Christian life. If I hold on to my little self and never jump, I'm like a grain of wheat that refuses to leave the hopper and will never bear fruit. But if I offer myself up, how do I know I'm offering rightly? How do I know I'll end up seeing the face of God and not broken on the rocks below?

This is the free fall that the saints and the martyrs and you and I have to face before we can face God. It is terror.

It is also joy.

After the plummet, after the feeling that I have left my stomach and probably my brain several hundred feet behind, I will find myself caught and held by the everlasting arms and set gently down on new ground, in a new kingdom, to begin a new life.

I stand on the edge of the cliff and remember
that you said that you are not willing
that any should perish.
I will trust you and let go. Catch me, Lord;
I rely on only you.

CHAPTER SEVENTEEN

What a Difference an S Makes

There's a phrase that strikes me whenever I hear it. It appears every week in the Orthodox liturgy and occasionally in the Catholic one: it is "Father of lights," as in "Every good gift and every perfect gift is from above, coming down from the Father of lights."

After a lifetime of reading and hearing Scripture, I accept without question and even without thought that God is light: the light that we see, and the light by which we see. It's a good image and illustrates God's nature well. But still, light is abstract, vast, a physical conundrum of molecular particles hurtling through space, composed of all colors or none—I don't understand it. It blinds me as often as it helps me see.

But the "s" in the phrase "Father of lights" changes the image of God in my mind. Lights—plural—are not vast and incomprehensible but domestic and cozy. *Light* is something that only Einstein and the great mystics could look at directly; *lights*, on the other hand, are all around me. They are the uncreated light of God coming down as candle flames, reading lamps, and headlights on the highway.

That little "s" unites the ineffable immensities with our daily experience. It refutes Gnosticism and other dualistic misunderstandings. God is vast and distant, yes, but also intimately among us. God's brilliance is not lost or tempered in this fallen world. The blessing of light is the same whether in the sun or in a flashlight. As Dante described so beautifully in *Paradiso*, our capacities to reflect light may vary, but light itself is perfect, the ultimate good thing coming down from above.

God, if you are the Father of lights, then I see your hand everywhere. It is by your will that water, ruffled by wind, casts reflections of light on the underside of leaves. You ordain that on summer evenings, fireflies hover above the farm fields, flickering like phosphorescence on the surface of the sea. You set the dust motes spinning in the sunbeam and cause the light from evening windows to make a path across the snow. You are in every spiderweb pearled with dew and every puddle lit by the reflections of neon signs.

You must also have been in this scene: My five-year-old daughter and I were walking home from the bazaar in Kyrgyzstan with our groceries. Our path led us through a field behind an abandoned hotel where the alcoholics hung out at night. The ground was covered in shards of glass from broken vodka bottles. I was picking my way distastefully through the garbage when I heard my daughter gasp, "Look how pretty it is!" I glanced up and saw through her eyes the hundreds of lights where the sun caught the broken glass, sparkling like jewels. I had to beat back the impulse to explain to her that no, it wasn't pretty; it was disgusting. Because she was right—the Father of lights had created beauty out of trash.

Lord of lights,
you fill heaven but do not scorn
the bleak places of this world.
Darkness flees from you,
and even the meanest things
in some way reflect your brightness.
Shine your lights for me
in the deepest shadows of my life.
Amen.

CHAPTER EIGHTEEN

Consider It All Joy

My family and I were missionaries in Kyrgyzstan for some years. Our furloughs in America were busy and tiring. We had to pack too frequently, try to keep the children sane, and say the same things a hundred times to people we'd mostly never see again. The summer I'm thinking about was a particularly difficult one.

I was asked to speak to one more women's group at a church that supported us. They were lovely people. They all wanted to know about my work overseas and my spiritual life. Many of them presumed my spiritual life was triumphant—I was a missionary, after all. I spoke about the struggles of Christians in Kyrgyzstan and the challenges of our work. Afterwards, they went around the circle and told what they thought about my message. Again and again they spoke of joy—how joyful I seemed, and how joyful they felt listening to me.

Joyful? Not me. I'm often impatient, discontented, and critical. I was not aware at that time of feeling joyful. My first (silent) reaction was, "These women have no insight or are just lying to be polite." I told you I was critical.

But then a blinding realization occurred to me: maybe they were right and I was wrong. Maybe they saw joy, if not in me, then through me. Perhaps God was working through me in a way that others were more aware of than I was. If so, what they saw was God's joy, not mine.

Then joy must not be just a feeling, since I wasn't aware of feeling it. What was joy?

The common understanding is happiness, expressed as cheerfulness. But most of the holiest people in Scripture and Christian history don't seem to be unflaggingly smiley. Many of the saints lived hardscrabble lives of poverty and pain. Joy is mentioned in the Bible many times, but it doesn't seem to be equated with comfort or happiness or freedom from troubles.

In the days following that meeting, I considered if there was anything genuine I could claim, if not joy. Only one thing occurred to me. Those years in the mission field, when I felt uncomfortable, frustrated, overworked, and isolated, when I had rocks thrown at me and the windows of my house smashed, my goal was at least obedience. I was told to die to myself daily, and God provided me with daily opportunities to do that. It didn't feel joyful to me at all; it felt, in fact, like death.

But what if obedience is the same thing as joy but only looks different from the inside and outside? I started flipping through the concordance to see how obedience and joy were related in Scripture.

"If you keep my commandments, you will abide in my love, just as I have kept my Father's commandments and abide in his love," says Jesus. "These things I have spoken to you, that my joy may be in you, and that your joy may be full" (JOHN 15:10–11).

In Matthew 25:21, Jesus concludes a parable with *"Well done, good and faithful servant. You have been faithful over a little, I will set you over much; enter into the joy of your master."*

The writer of Hebrews exhorts us to "… run with perseverence the race that is set before us, looking to Jesus, the pioneer and perfector of our faith, who for the joy that was set before him endured the cross" (**HEBREWS 12:1B–2A**).

And James says, "Count it all joy, brethren, when you meet various trials, for you know that the testing of your faith produces steadfastness" (**JAMES 1:2–3**).

I concluded that joy isn't a feeling or a thing we have; it's almost more of a place, one that we're invited to enter into and abide in. Joy is the keeping of God's commandments; it is faithfulness in discharging duties. It's the result of endurance, and also the reason for it.

Many of us are suffering these days. We struggle with families, jobs or lack of them, church, health—you can add your own list. The happy-clappy Christian culture tells us to be joyful. Are we supposed to be hypocrites? We can't always be cheerful. But we can obey. We can be faithful. We can endure. And we can abide in joy.

Sing praise to the Lord, you saints of his,
and give thanks at the remembrance of his holy name.
For his anger is but for a moment,
his favor is for life;
weeping may endure for a night,
but joy comes in the morning.

You have turned for me my mourning into dancing;

you have put off my sackcloth and clothed me with gladness,
to the end that my glory may sing praise to you and not be silent.
O Lord my God, I will give thanks to you forever.

(PSALM 30:4–5, 11–12)

CHAPTER NINETEEN

Filled with Passionate Intensity

D oes anyone else cringe when they hear the overused word "passion"? "What's your passion?" "I have a passion for"—something. "I'm so passionate about that." I don't think these people know what they're really saying. Bear with me while I pick apart the word.

Passion comes from the Latin word meaning to suffer. There are two meanings combined in both the Latin and the English. One is simply to endure or be the recipient of action, to be passive. The other is to experience pain.

The first meaning of passion in the *Oxford English Dictionary* is generally capitalized. It means Jesus' suffering before and during the crucifixion. It may by extension mean the gospel narratives referring to his suffering, or it may even be a piece of music on the same topic, such as Bach's *St. Matthew Passion*.

Next, it can mean the suffering of any martyr, or the suffering brought on by any affliction or disease.

These are not what modern Christians mean when they refer to their passion for orphans or for teaching Bible studies or for scrapbooking for the Lord.

The second category of meaning in the OED is "the fact of being acted upon by external agency, being passive, being subject to external force." Do the people who boast of their strong feelings for a particular calling mean to imply that they are passive and are possessed or propelled by some outside force? What outside force would that be?

The OED then moves to the more familiar usages: "an affection of the mind; a feeling by which the mind is powerfully moved or acted upon." It goes on to "an abandonment to emotions," "angry or amorous feelings," and "sexual desire."

Finally, it arrives at the meaning we commonly hear in modern Christian circles: "an eager outreaching of the mind toward something; an overmastering zeal or enthusiasm;" or as a noun, "an aim or object pursued with zeal."

Several things are common to all these definitions. First is the strength of feeling involved, whether it's presumed to be a pleasant or an unpleasant feeling. Second is the "passivity" of the person experiencing the feeling. We speak of being moved as a synonym for feeling passionate, and it's a good synonym. The OED uses the words "acted upon," "abandonment," and "overmastering" in its definitions of passion, also implying a loss of control or a loss of self.

What do people think they're really saying when they claim to be passionate about something? Are they implying that the strength of their feelings determines the value of the object or pursuit? Or do they mean that the strength of their feelings witnesses to the fineness and devotion of their own characters? I think they're often saying both.

Generally, people who have a passion think well of themselves for having it. Linguistically they are comparing their interest in their current spiritual hobby with the suffering of Jesus and the deaths of the martyrs. But was passion the foundation for the obedience of the martyrs or the total self-emptying of Christ? We know that in human relationships, passion is usually the opposite of committed longevity. No, the passion of the martyrs or Jesus means not the fervor with which they faced suffering but the suffering that came about because of their faithfulness. That's not what someone means who begins a conversation with "So—what's your passion?"

To me, the proclaiming of a passion sounds like boasting. I don't know that I'm right to think so in every case. Many people who declare they're passionate about something are just using the accepted phrase without considering what they're saying. But some people who "have a passion" are definitely trying to trump others who are humbly obeying God's word and finding God's work. Boasting of passion, however, is a dangerous boast. As I mentioned above, one aspect of "passion" is being acted upon by an external agent. These boasters may not think so, but they're saying that they are under compulsion from some source, that they are being moved, or driven, to feel as they do. Let's remember that strong feelings and external compulsions are not solely the attribute of the good. The poet Yeats reminds us that "the worst are filled with passionate intensity."

You may think that I'm blowing this out of proportion. The huge majority of people who talk about their passion don't mean any of the things I'm saying, nor do they know about the etymology of the word. They just mean that they **care** a lot about something.

But even that's tricky. I often find that the things I care most about, that I'm most passionate about, are not the things that God cares most about. Some of my most passionate prayers have been answered with a resounding "No!" Saint Paul found the same thing. He prayed three times, he said, to have his affliction removed from him. God told him no, that God's purposes will be accomplished in God's own way, that God's "power is made perfect in weakness." Not Paul's passion but God's will determined what was right and important.

To the church fathers, passion, or zeal, was a bad thing. Passions were uncontrollable forces that you suffered. If they weren't sins themselves, they were at least temptations to sins. The passionate man never dwelt in God's peace. He was like the children described by Saint Paul in Ephesians 4:14, "tossed back and forth by the waves, and blown here and there by every wind of teaching and by the cunning and craftiness of men in their deceitful scheming."

Saint Isaac of Syria, one of my favorites among the Fathers, says this:

> A zealous [or passionate] person never achieves peace of mind. And he who is deprived of peace is deprived of joy.

> If, as is said, peace of mind is perfect health, and zeal is opposed to peace, then a person stirred by zeal is ill with a grievous sickness.

> Zeal is not reckoned among mankind as a form of wisdom; rather it is one of the sicknesses of the soul, arising from narrow-mindedness and deep ignorance.

> The beginning of divine wisdom is the serenity acquired from generosity of soul and forbearance with human infirmities.

(FROM *DAILY READINGS WITH SAINT ISAAC OF SYRIA*,
EDITED BY A.M. ALLCHIN AND TRANSLATED
BY SEBASTIAN BROCK)

Passion and soul-sickness on the one hand? Divine wisdom and
serenity on the other? I'll choose Door Number Two.

Lord, may I rest in you
like a weaned child on its mother's breast.
May I find peace in knowing
that I don't have to rely
on the combustion of passion
as the motivating power of the Christian life,
but that I can trust you to lead me in quietness.
Amen.

CHAPTER TWENTY

=[CHAPTER TWENTY]=

How We Become Human

I know, as a tenet of my faith, that Jesus' incarnation, death, and resurrection have set me free from death and given me new life. I know that God promises to take away my heart of stone and give me a heart of flesh. But I don't understand how that happens or even how it looks in human terms. Recently, though, I may have gotten a glimpse at part of the process.

Our normal pew at church is more than halfway around the Stations of the Cross, which are displayed up and down the side walls. On the other side of the church, bas-relief panels show the earliest steps leading up to the Crucifixion, but where I sit, the scenes show Jesus stumbling and falling, wounded and exhausted. I really don't like looking at them and usually turn my eyes away. Sometimes the depictions make me feel angry, sometimes depressed and disgusted with the whole human race. But on a recent morning, for some reason, my usual defenses were breached. I looked closely at the images of Jesus collapsed and crushed, and I felt pity, overwhelming pity, for—well, for God.

It seemed like hubris to pity the Lord of all, as if I were above him somehow and condescending to him. Then I remembered the trial depicted in *To Kill a Mockingbird*. Tom Robinson, a black man falsely accused of raping a white woman, was asked why he had approached and interacted with her. "I felt sorry for her," he said—and we know at that moment that Tom was doomed regardless of the facts of the case. That a black man would dare to feel sorry for a white woman—poor trash or not—was insupportable to the all-white jury. Tom, being black, could not be thought of as human in the same way they were. They could not stand the realization that pity made Tom Robinson truly human in a way that most people in the courtroom weren't. In that aspect he was like Jesus, who pitied the people who had it in their power to put him to death.

It occurred to me, in the quick glances at the Stations of the Cross that were all I could endure: Christ gave himself to us partly *in order to be pitied*. The maker of the universe, the Holy, the Almighty, became a baby and a victim of our sin and injustice so that we would pity him. Maybe my pity is the first sign that my heart of stone is turning into flesh. Maybe my new life is not just the result of Christ conquering death, which inspires feelings of gratitude and joy. The new life is also being bought for me daily by his weakness and suffering, which inspire me to pity God himself.

I consider your deep humility, Lord, and pray:
Melt my heart of stone
and make me truly human.
Amen.

CHAPTER TWENTY-ONE

The Crossroads

few years ago, at Easter, my family and I joined the Catholic Church. Each of us would phrase our reasons for doing so somewhat differently, but here are a few of mine.

When my husband and I told an old friend that we had begun going to the Catholic Church, he said, "Well, I'm glad you've found a place that feels like home." My husband immediately responded, "No, we've found a place that feels like *church*!" Our parish gathers in silence and prayer, focuses on the Bible and the Eucharist, and conducts itself with joyful solemnity through the liturgy.

I like the liturgy of the Catholic Church. Liturgy means "the work of the people." Liturgical worship is not the work of the leader; it is not a spectator sport, or a concert, or a pep rally. Liturgy reminds us of our place in the scheme of things. I am not in charge. I am a servant and an heir to the faith that has been handed down to me. The priest himself is the servant of the liturgy, not its boss.

So my family and I feel security in knowing that a new pastor is not going to change entirely what we had known as good. There will be changes, but the essential things will remain the same. We did not experience this security in the shifting world of evangelicalism.

I like the universality of the Catholic Church. Universality doesn't just mean that the Mass will be the same anywhere on the planet, although that is true. It also means that we joined *the* church, not *a* church. Our parish of several hundred people *is* the Catholic Church. It's not a part or fraction of it; it's not a local franchise of it. Each parish is fully the church. The best analogy I can think of is that the church is like the ocean. Each community knows a particular bay or beach or bank, but the ocean is still the ocean in its entirety wherever we experience it. Certain other understandings of church, the Baptist one, for example, suggest that congregations are more like discrete islands. In some cases they are even different countries where people require visas and change of citizenship to move among them.

I like the incarnational theology of the Catholic Church. I can't say I fathom the depths of what happens in the Eucharist or in any of the sacraments, but they match what I know of God. The astounding, central fact of God's relationship with us is the Incarnation. God became human. In the person of Jesus he took on human flesh and dwelled with us. He was fully human and fully divine. Evidently, matter can be imbued with divinity, not changing the substance of either the matter or the divinity. As a Christian, I believe that that happened once, two thousand years ago. As a Catholic Christian, I also accept that that is God's regular mode of revelation. If Christ can be both matter and God, then through him so can bread and wine. Water can be both water and new birth. Oil can be both oil and blessing.

What a rich world incarnational theology opens up for us! Matter reveals the Immaterial. The beauty of creation around us, properly seen, is not a distraction or temptation—it is "charged with the grandeur of God," as Gerard Manley Hopkins put it. When our desires are rightly ordered, we are not faced with "either/or" but always "both/and." We are given both God and creation, both saving grace and common grace. Everything has meaning, and everything points us to God.

I like the balance of Catholic theology. Some Christians hold that all the work—and therefore responsibility—of salvation rests with God alone. I can't entirely reconcile that view with the commands and exhortations of Jesus Christ as recorded in the gospels. Others claim that people have the power to commend themselves to God in their own strength. I can't reconcile that view with St. Paul's epistles. The best summary of the dual nature of our salvation is in Philippians 2:12–13: "continue to work out your salvation with fear and trembling, for it is God who works in you to will and to act according to his good purposes." I trust the Catholic understanding of the ongoing nature of salvation and the necessity for both grace and work.

I don't think that the Catholic Church is perfect, either in its parochial or universal aspects. Not all of its doctrines commend themselves to my understanding, at this point at least, nor do all of its practices commend themselves to my taste or even my conscience. And I wish that, in addition to the crucifix displayed in every church, there was also an icon of the resurrection.

But it feels like church. It smells like church. It's been church for so long.

This is what the Lord says:
Stand at the crossroads and look;
ask for the ancient paths,
ask where the good way is, and walk in it,
and you will find rest for your souls.
(JEREMIAH 6:16)

CHAPTER TWENTY-TWO

Your Dwelling Place

"How lovely is your dwelling place, O Lord of Hosts!"
(PSALM 84:1)

What is the dwelling place of the Lord? It can be a Gothic cathedral, surging upward like flames, like trees drawing their strength from the ground and flowering into a hundred branches far overhead. The stained glass scatters bright jewels of color on stone. The cathedral points upward, saying, "Lift your eyes and look to the heavens: who created all these?"

Or a Byzantine basilica, where heaven is not pointed to but enclosed beneath the dome, within the arms of Christ *Pantokrator*. A cloud of incense veils the cloud of witnesses peering through the icons, the windows of heaven.

Or a Quaker meeting house, empty and clean, like a shell scoured by the sea. Bare wood, plain lines restful to the eye, lit by the happy light pouring through windows. Silence, peace.

How lovely is your dwelling place, O Lord of Hosts.

"I was glad when they said unto me, let us go into the house of the Lord" (Psalm 122:1). I have known churches in many places—rough benches beneath a scaffolding of palm fronds in Africa, mats on the floor of a chilly one-room house in the mountains of Central Asia, wooden pews filling a white clapboard building in New England, a village church in Bavaria rippling with gilded ranks of rococo angels.

I remember a tiny whitewashed church on a Greek hillside—a dome on a box. Inside, a few candles flicker; their flames are reflected by small metal plaques hanging next to the icons. The image on each plaque represents what the petitioner is praying for: a child, a car, an arm.

The white light outside the church is blinding, glorious. The Greek hillside is also God's dwelling place. "The earth is the Lord's and the fullness thereof" (Psalm 24:1; 1 Corinthians 10:26). Surely the Lord delights in the smell of thyme and sea as much as in incense; surely God's presence is announced as compellingly by the clunk of sheep bells as by the clangor of a carillon.

Or a forest where light falls through the branches—this is God's dwelling place too. The immensity of plains or sea, the strength of mountains, sky, sun, stars, and moon: "If I go to the heavens, you are there; if I make my bed in the depths, you are there. If I rise on the wings of the dawn, if I settle on the far side of the sea, even there your hand will guide me, your right hand will hold me fast" (Psalm 139:8–10).

But we are small, and we mostly can't endure the immensities of creation. On Sunday morning, we rejoice to go to the house of the Lord. It's a plain building, perhaps. There are children crying, people wrestling with coats, doors opening and closing. There may be no great artwork inside and only a tangle of city streets outside. But our churches are built on Jesus' promise:

"Behold, I stand at the door and knock. If anyone hears my voice and opens the door, I will come in and eat with him, and he with me" (Revelation 3:20). And we build the church so that we can open the door and he can come in.

One evangelical church building I saw looked like a pole barn. There were no hangings, no stained glass, no color or beauty. The carpeted dais and the floor around it were a snakepit of electrical wires. Duct tape disfigured floor and walls. Empty water bottles lay here and there, and microphone stands stuck up randomly like snags in a swamp. It had all the beauty of a field after the circus has left. Where was God?

Then the people began to pour in. Plain people, just parents with kids, teenagers, old people. They were talking, laughing, even calling to each other as they took their seats, like a mob of crows settling onto their branches for the night. And suddenly I really saw them: they "are the temple of the living God; as God has said, 'I will live in them and move among them, and I will be their God, and they shall be my people'" (2 Corinthians 6:16).

How lovely is your dwelling place, O Lord of Hosts!

In a mystery, in the between time, God already dwells among us—in our church buildings, in creation, in the church, and in each believer—yet we still await the Advent. With John we pray, "Come, Lord Jesus" (Revelation 22:20). And God answers us, "'The virgin will be with child and will give birth to a son, and they will call him Immanuel'—which means, 'God with us'" (Matthew 1:23).

How lovely is your dwelling place,
O Lord of hosts!
My soul longs, yes, faints
for the courts of the Lord;
my heart and flesh sing for joy
to the living God.

Even the sparrow finds a home,
 and the swallow a nest for herself,
 where she may lay her young,
at your altars, O Lord of hosts,
 my King and my God.
Blessed are those who dwell in your house,
 ever singing your praise!
(PSALM 84:1–4)

Amen.